LONELY,
BUT NEVER ALONE

LONELY,
BUT NEVER ALONE

NICKY CRUZ

with Madalene Harris

ZONDERVAN
PUBLISHING HOUSE OF THE ZONDERVAN CORPORATION
GRAND RAPIDS, MICHIGAN 49506

LONELY, BUT NEVER ALONE
Copyright © 1981 by The Zondervan Corporation
Grand Rapids, Michigan

Library of Congress Cataloging in Publication Data

Cruz, Nicky.
    Lonely, but never alone.

    Includes bibliographical references.
    1. Loneliness. 2. Cruz, Nicky. I. Harris, Madalene, 1925–
joint author. II. Title.
BV4911.C79   248.8'6   80-28456
ISBN 0-310-43362-2

Designed and edited by Edward Viening

Printed in the United States of America

83 84 85 86 87 88 — 10 9 8 7 6 5 4 3

Dedication

I am very happy and proud to dedicate this book to the staff of the Nicky Cruz Girls' Home. These young women are the little people behind the scenes: the ones you never hear about. They have dealt with immeasurable problems throughout the years and have always been dedicated and committed to their work. I can honestly say that they are a tremendous blessing and strength to this ministry.

This book is dedicated to:

June Creswell, Director
Fay Biddle, Assistant Director
Bett Blackwood
Sharlene Creech
Cathy Rawlinson
Sandy Thompson
Mary Wilson
and the rest of the staff.

Contents

Acknowledgments

I would like to express my sincere appreciation to all the people who did research and work for this book. I do not have the words to show my thanks and gratitude:

To June Creswell: who gave me some material on loneliness.

To Sandy Thompson: who started the work on the manuscript, and spent many long hours typing and proofreading.

To Cathy Rawlinson: my personal secretary, who worked an unlimited amount of hours, both day and night, retyping the script, putting the pieces together, and preparing the final copy for the publisher.

Appreciation

I first met Madalene Harris when my family and I moved from Raleigh, North Carolina to Colorado Springs, Colorado. This move affected my wife, Gloria, and our four children far more than it did me because I was almost always gone on crusades leaving them alone much of the time. Madalene Harris, having heard that we were in town, came to our front door the second day of our traumatic displacement with a warm welcome for my family.

I soon discovered Madalene's capabilities as a writer as I read her recent book, *The Moon Is Not Enough.* From its success, I could see she was a very gifted writer.

One day I shared with her my ideas about a book on loneliness that I had been planning for three years. She became excited and began to pray for God's blessing on me in this endeavor. With my extensive crusade schedule, however, I knew I would not be able to accomplish the writing alone. I began to pray for God's leadership as to our working together. Little did I know at the time I was praying, that soon Madalene would be helping me in this new venture.

We quickly developed a close working relationship and discovered as the months moved along that we were "one spirit" in the Lord. I praise the Lord for Madalene Harris because she was a unique answer to prayer—and also because she is a tremendous writer. Thank you, Madalene.

Nicky Cruz

LONELY,
BUT NEVER ALONE

Prologue

WHO REALLY CARES?

The uneven lettering in bright green paint splashed carelessly across a huge board fence in a rundown section of New York City interrupted my preoccupied reverie. Twenty minutes earlier I had landed at bustling Kennedy Airport, had flagged a taxi, and was being transported to the New York Hilton Hotel to do a television special with Art Linkletter—"No Need to Hide." My thoughts were centered on the task ahead, and I was almost oblivious to my surroundings—when suddenly, there it was. It was impossible to escape the pathetic cry of an anonymous passer-by who could contain no longer the utter loneliness and emptiness of his or her soul. The anguish the painter suffered sought some kind of release so the message was painted in gigantic, awkward-looking letters where everyone could see.

Unexpectedly, the taxi driver let out a torrent of the foulest language I had heard in many a day. A careless driver had cut in front of him forcing him to slam on his brakes and skid several feet to avoid a collision. It was as if a sewer had opened and he couldn't stop the flow of filth. He turned to me as if to seek confirmation. The jammed, bumper-to-bumper rush-hour traffic, the intense heat of the muggy July afternoon without air conditioning, the stench of the inner city, and the poignant plea of that time-worn fence had gotten to me. I looked the driver straight in the eye and angrily said, "You need Listerine in your mouth, buddy. You can just stop this cab right now and let me out. I don't want anymore of your garbage."

He stared at me for a moment in utter disbelief, then rather mechanically pulled his vehicle over to the curb and stopped. Handing him a $10 bill, I scrambled out and waved down another cab. Soon we were inching our way down the Van Wyck Expressway, through Midtown Tunnel under the East River, and finally pulled up in front of the

Hilton on 6th Avenue and 53rd Street. Not a word of conversation passed between this cabbie and myself.

The taping session wouldn't begin until morning, so I checked into my room on the 32nd floor and tried to rest, but there was no rest in me. Soon I was pacing the floor and wondering what to do with myself. *Maybe I'm hungry,* I thought. The streets of New York City aren't safe for anyone to be walking at night, I knew only too well, and by now it was almost 11:00 P.M. For many years I had been a part of the muggings and robberies that kept people in constant horror day and night, so no one needed to tell me about it. Now that I was on the other side of the violence, the hotel restaurant was as far as I dared venture.

Back in my room after a steak dinner, still restless, I drew back my draperies to a magnificent sight. High above the honking cars and deafening roar of traffic, the filth and grime of city streets, I was in another world. A thousand twinkling diamonds lighted in the Americana Hotel windows across the way, the fabled New York skyline was ablaze against the black horizon, and the miniature cars silently creeping below bore no resemblance to the New York I knew.

The longer I looked, the angrier I became. My plush surroundings, the $12 steak I had just eaten, and the beautiful, but unrealistic picture out the window was not New York.

With the inner eye piercing through this insulated facade, I looked down on a forgotten people living in condemned buildings amidst filth, hunger, and squalor unknown to most Americans. I saw the despairing drug addicts, hopeless alcoholics and winos, the greedy pimps, and lonely street walkers. I felt their heartbeat. I knew their despair. Most of them never would have the opportunity to walk away from that miserable hell on earth, and although it was the only life they had ever known, they hated it and dreamed of something better. The longer I stood at the window, the more certain I was that I did not belong in these luxurious surroundings. But I didn't belong to the ghetto either. I could never return to it, but neither could I abandon it. Where did I really belong?

Suddenly those forgotten people beckoned, and in a moment's time I had changed clothes and found myself in another taxi heading toward my old neighborhood. It wasn't long before I had located Jose, a friend of those former days—days when I roamed the streets as a leader of the most feared and bloodthirsty street gangs in New York City. Still a drug addict, Jose was a pathetic sight. He was hungry, broke, and lonely. By now it was 2:00 A.M., so I took him to a nearby coffee shop and drank coffee while he ate.

As I carefully watched Jose, our eyes finally met, and I broke the silence by asking, "How ya doin', Jose?"

"Awright," he answered slowly.

"How is your wife?" I ventured further.

"Juanita? She's livin'," he shrugged. "Just livin'."

I knew what he meant. Existing. Barely existing would have been more accurate. Those cheap, tiny holes of apartments where countless Jose's and Juanita's passed weary days and hopeless nights were still vivid in my mind.

"Do you have a job, Jose?" I decided not to probe family matters any deeper.

"Come on, Nicky," he growled. "What would I be doing here in the middle of the night if I had a job? I'd be in bed asleep."

As I looked into his despondent eyes, I thought I had never seen such hopelessness. It was like the crying out of a man who had punished himself with so much sin in his life that there was nothing left.

Feeling Jose's despair gripping my own heart, I decided to strike a lighter vein. "How many children do you have?" I laughed as I added, "Let's see now, knowing us Latins, you should have about eight."

For the first time a grin crossed his weary countenance.

"Only two. To tell you the truth, I'm not home much anymore. My home is the streets, you know."

Glancing at my watch, I noted that the time was 2:30 A.M. "Is it too late to go see your wife?" I asked.

"No, no, not at all." I could tell he meant it. "Whenever I talk about you, Nicky, she always says she wants to meet you. Come on, let's go."

As we walked down the street, blackened except for the yellow glare of street lights on each block, I began asking about my old friends—guys who had been a part of our gang. Many were dead—killed by the police or enemy gangs. Most who survived were like Jose. Drug addicts. Winos. Shiftless. A few, however, brought joy to my heart. Like Israel, who had trusted Christ when I did and was living for Jesus.

Suddenly Jose changed the subject. "Nicky, the town is dying. Look around. It's a lot worse than when you were here." After a long silence, he continued. "Even worse is that the people are dying, too. And worse than that, I'm dying with them."

At that point I was glad we had arrived at the front of the old tenement building where Jose lived. Walking into his apartment, I saw his wife, looking dismal, sitting in a chair, smoking a cigarette, and listening to Latin music. She was dressed in a long robe, her face was washed free of cosmetics, and I was amazed at her natural beauty. A pure, flawless complexion was set off by deepset, dark Spanish eyes and was framed with lustrous black hair; she could have been a fashion model. Glancing again at Jose's dissipated appearance, I wondered what held these two together.

Juanita looked up without a sign of expression on her face.

"You know who this is?" Jose asked.

"How would I know? I've never seen him before," came the flat reply.

"It's Nicky. Nicky Cruz. Remember, I told you about him?"

I was unprepared for her reaction. She jumped off the chair, threw her arms around me, and hugged me. I was not to understand this unexpected gesture until a little later.

"I'm so happy to meet you at last," her expressionless eyes now sparkled. "Jose has told me so much about you."

"Come see the children," she urged. Her eyes beckoned, and she could not conceal her pride.

Although the children were fast asleep, we tiptoed into their bedroom. She motioned to the little sleeping forms. How sweet and innocent they were lying there. I thought of my own precious little girls, safe in clean beds surrounded by their dolls and toys, with plenty of food and an opportunity to grow up to a fulfilling life. What had these children done to deserve being born into this?

"I'm surprised to see my man," Juanita finally said after she closed the bedroom door.

"Juanita, Jose really loves you. I know he does," I tried to assure her. "He just has a lot of problems, you know."

"Maybe." She committed herself no further.

"Let me fix you some Puerto Rican coffee, Nicky." She led the way into the kitchen. Strangely, I did not feel the least bit ill at ease. They were so glad to see me that I was comfortable and at home immediately.

Jose started laughing as he recalled the old days. "Remember that time you almost got killed, Nicky, when we were in a rumble?"

How well I remembered the switchblade poking my stomach when Jose rescued me.

We continued to reminisce a little longer, then I cleared my throat and slowly began in another direction. "Through all of that, I don't know, Jose—I should have been dead. It's a wonderful privilege to be alive."

Jose narrowed his eyes as if to look straight through me. "You happy, Nicky? I'm not."

"I want to tell you something, Jose. I don't have to talk about the old days, old times—I didn't prove anything by being tough, macho. It almost cost *my* life, *your* life, everybody's life, and you know, Jose, we were all hurting inside. Someway, somehow, we didn't want to be the people we were on the streets—robbing, mugging, murdering. And you don't want to be the guy you are right now."

He was listening intently, so I continued. "You know, Jose, one of your biggest problems is that you're using stuff—drugs. And the thing I can't understand is that Juanita accepts what you are, and she's still with you."

At that Juanita grabbed him and put her arms around him. "This damn woman loves me so much. I don't deserve it. I've stolen money from her children and from her; I took her jewelry and sold it. I've given her nothing but misery. And she still loves me and goes to church twice a week to burn a candle for me so someday I'll be a good guy." He shook his head as he spoke. "You know, Nicky, whenever I mention your name, she always says, 'Why don't you be good like Nicky?'"

Now I knew why I was here. "Look, Jose, it's Jesus in me that makes the difference, and it is only Jesus in you that can make a difference. It doesn't matter how we look. It's not physical appearance, where we come from, whether we are rich or poor or whatever. It's Jesus, Jose, and He's here in this room right now. I came over here tonight to honor Jesus."

Tears came to my eyes, and Juanita started crying, too. "Jesus might hate everything you're doing, Jose—cheating, lying, stealing—*but He really does love you, Juanita, and the children.*"

Jose broke down and cried. "We want peace in this hell, Nicky. We want peace in the midst of this rotten city."

Right there in that little tenement kitchen we had a beautiful prayer. Both Jose and Juanita asked Jesus into their lives, and when they looked up, their eyes shone. I knew the miracle of new life had happened. They would never be the same.

"Nicky," Jose spoke with a choked voice, "you must go back into the bedroom and bless the children."

"I'm not the pope, Jose. I can't bless your children or anyone else. But I can pray for them," I added.

The three of us crept back to the little beds, knelt together, and whispered a prayer as I laid a hand on each of the sleeping forms.

Driving back to the Hilton just before dawn, the earlier restlessness within had subsided and I was at peace with myself. Being with Jose and Juanita was a release. It made me thankful—oh, so thankful for the miracle, the mercy, the love of Jesus Christ. When I travel so much, hotel after hotel, cities, states, countries, I move so fast and so constantly that I don't have time to think of myself. Going back made me see, just in case I had forgotten, that I was a nobody. Only the love of God had lifted me from that stinking hell and changed me.

Once again in my room, I could look out the window with a different perspective. As the first rosy tint of daybreak appeared on the eastern sky I began to reflect on the day's events, and a conviction that had been growing in my spirit for two years now intensified the compelling need for action. My entire life had been characterized by early parental rejection, feelings of misplacement in every environment, and the resultant loneliness such rejection brings. For years I suspected that my inner loneliness was unique to my unusual background, but as my crusade ministry widened and was now touching the lives of thousands of people, I was discovering that loneliness is universal. Thomas Wolfe expressed this discovery succinctly when he wrote: "The whole conviction of my life now rests upon the belief that loneliness, far from being a rare and curious phenomenon peculiar to myself and to a few other solitary men, is the central and inevitable fact of human existence."[1]

If that be so, I knew I had a responsibility before God and the people I served to address this need and alleviate in some measure its debilitating malignancy. Because I knew there were answers, for I had found some of them, I needed to communicate them on a wider scale than just personal contacts; therefore, writing this book seemed the only solution.

While others may deal with the problem of loneliness on a much deeper level psychologically, I will not use this approach. In the simplest terms available, so that all who read may understand, I shall present throughout this book my own experiences and the solutions I found. Wherever possible, I will include practical applications so that you may relate the material to your individual circumstances.

I discovered during the first seventeen years of my life that the loneliest of all conditions is that of being without the love of God through Jesus Christ. To be spiritually lost is to experience the deepest of alienations, which is eternal separation from the God who created us and loves us unconditionally. The first few chapters will be directed to this plight.

I learned, however, much to my dismay, that you can be a Christian and still be lonely. In my own experience, when finally I heard the message of God's love for lonely sinners and responded by receiving Jesus Christ as my personal Savior, I made the common mistake of assuming that God's children are loving and perfect. *We are all brothers and sisters in the family of God,* I joyously concluded, *and I won't be lonely anymore.*

What a disillusioning process to learn, after being almost totally rejected by the Christian community into which I was thrust, that Christians are not perfect—only forgiven. The initial step of faith that changes our relationship to God and places us in the body of Christ is identified in one biblical account as being "born again," so the comparison of spiritual birth to physical birth implies the necessary process of growth. An important facet of this process is learning to love each other, and through loving relationships to overcome loneliness. Instead of being inwardly destroyed, then, and rendered ineffective in our Christian lives, we can become powerfully secure and untouched by the ravages of loneliness.

The rest of the book is designed to provide solutions to loneliness for Christians, so read on, and let's whip this giant.

Part I

The Unsaved Heart Is a Lonely Hunter

1

Does Anyone Care About Me?

Loneliness has many names—delinquency, alcoholism, psychiatric problems, physical illness, drug addiction, nervous breakdown, suicide, divorce. We often identify only symptoms and fail to diagnose the underlying cause or causes, blaming instead overwork, stress, incompatibility, wrong companions, bad environment, and a host of contributing factors, when the real culprit, loneliness, goes undetected and untreated.

We seldom think of little children experiencing loneliness, but we are told that loneliness begins in a person when he or she is very young. Ira J. Tanner in his book *Loneliness: The Fear of Love* wrote, "Loneliness has its beginnings in childhood sometime between the ages of one and three. It is a root condition of life and it is during these post-embryonic years that we first begin to experience doubt as to our self worth."[1]

Our problem is that we easily ignore or dismiss the whole idea of childhood loneliness in our busy pursuit of life. With so much emphasis on status, education, materialism, and social involvement, our consciences are pacified if we feel we have provided for our children those things we consider necessities, and even many luxuries. Children do not know they are lonely when parents seem too busy to enter their small worlds, and parents seldom recognize the possible basis of unacceptable behavior, chronic stomach aches, or various attention-seeking devices. The child may be saying, "I'm lonely. Please love me."

My own bitter trauma and lifelong struggle against loneliness began at an early age. I was too young to be able to identify my bewildering emotions in terms of rejection, denial, exclusion, meaninglessness. I only knew that no one cared. How did I know?

Among my earliest recollections are two incidents that the passing years can never erase. I know now that my strong-willed father loved me in his own way. With seventeen children to feed and clothe, he could give little individual attention to us, and he probably never pondered deeply, if at all, the psychologically accepted methods of correcting his overwhelming brood. Survival was his only goal. At my age, however, I could neither understand nor interpret his actions in the light of his circumstances. All that concerned me were my own circumstances—and me, Nicky Cruz.

So when my father punished a childish disobedience by locking me in the pigeon house just before supper and leaving me there until bedtime in total darkness amidst angry, wildly fluttering birds that slammed against my body and the sides of the grimy shack, I knew without anyone telling me that my father could not love me.

"I hate you! I hate you!" I screamed into the echoless black of night. And I meant it. Hatred and rebellion pulsated through every inch of my small-for-its-age body.

Although I understood little about death, whatever it was, I wished for it. My inner rage was so intense that I knew if I had a knife, I could easily have plunged it into my body.

It seemed forever before my father finally came and

unlocked the door. Dragging me out of my darkened prison, he angrily said, "Now maybe you'll learn to mind your papa. Wash up and go to bed."

Hungry and frightened, I cried myself to sleep that night, tossing fitfully between nightmarish visions of flapping wings and pecking birds. I had not learned the lesson Papa intended.

The other incident involved my mother. To this day I do not fully understand her actions, but since both my parents were deeply engrossed in spiritism and the occult practices that thrived on the beautiful island of Puerto Rico, my birth place, their minds were often controlled by the powers of darkness. My father was a practicing witch and my mother a medium assisting her husband in all varieties of sorcery, magic, divination, exorcism, and communication with departed spirits. Because of my father's astounding ability to cast out demons and restore tormented victims to normalcy, he was lovingly called "the miracle worker," and was heralded throughout the island. People sought him from near and far, often traveling many miles for occult deliverance. Our big, hilltop house overlooked the tiny village of Las Piedras in the fertile valley below. It was a sort of headquarters in the area for psychic and supernatural activities. Two "spirit houses" adjoined the large house where Mama and Papa held seances and conducted much of their mysticism.

It was not unusual for Mama to be entertaining other mediums of the village during the hot, lazy afternoons, and it was not unusual for them to be interrupted by children. During such an afternoon gathering, my bouncing ball sent me scurrying into their midst to retrieve it. I was eight and in school, although I was small for my age. But it was sad how, at such a young age, I harbored such smoldering fires of rebellion and hatred.

"What a cute little boy Nicky is," one of the ladies remarked in my hearing. "He looks just like you, Alexandria. You must be proud of him."

Mama looked hard at me and began to sway in her chair, rocking back and forth. Her eyes rolled back into her head until only the whites showed. She held her arms straight out in front of her across the top of the table. Her fingers stiffened and quivered as she slowly raised her arms above her head and began to speak in a singsong tone of voice . . . "This . . . not . . . my . . . son. No, not Nicky. He never been mine. He child of greatest of all witches, Lucifer. No, not mine . . . son of satan, child of devil."[2]

Mama had obviously slipped into a trance. The chanting of her voice as it rose and fell frightened me. I dropped my ball and backed up against the wall, uncertain as to what might happen.

"Not mine . . . finger of satan on his soul . . . mark of beast touch his life . . . not mine," she continued.

As she spoke, great tears ran down her cheeks. Suddenly, however, she turned at me with wide eyes and shrieking voice. "Get away, devil! Get out of here. Do you hear? GET OUT!"

To my childish mind, her outburst, no matter how explainable in terms of spiritualism, could mean but one thing —she didn't love me.

Forgetting the ball that had silently rolled into some unseen corner, I did get out. Fast. My heart was pounding, and I became pale and choked. I knew she meant it, and as I sought refuge in a dark, secluded spot under our back-porch stairway, I felt like a china doll that had been thrown onto a concrete floor and broken into a thousand pieces. How I hated my mother!

After that experience, I feigned a semblance of obedience. It was my only safe course, for if I didn't obey, judgment would fall quickly. Inwardly, however, contempt for all authority boiled over, and as a result, I began to have problems in school as well as at home. Eventually, life became unbearable wherever I turned, so I made my plans to run away.

A small, nine-year-old boy could easily hide, I reasoned. So I quietly gathered up what food I could find while my mother was out shopping one day, slipped out of the house, headed down our hill on a concealed, seldom-used trail, toward the lush valley below. The little town of Humacao lay about five miles from Las Piedras. There I would be safe, I decided.

Oh, what ecstasy was mine! The exhilaration of the new-found freedom I experienced during that long walk offset my weariness. I finally found a little river nestled among thick tropical foliage and exotic flowers where I could dangle my bare feet in its refreshing waters and eat what food I had taken with me. That first day passed quickly. I didn't have to do chores; there was no one to order me around, and as dusk descended I knew I could go to bed whenever I wanted to, get up in the morning whenever I wanted to, and do exactly as I pleased in between. The warm Puerto Rican days and nights were ideal for this carefree existence, and sleeping under a sky scattered with sparkling stars was an exciting adventure to a young vagabond. For the first few days anyway.

When my food ran out, I found banana and mango trees, stole two large Spanish salami sausages and a long loaf of Puerto Rican bread. The third night, while I was sleeping, a stray dog snuggled up beside me, and in the morning light it was obvious by his bony, emaciated appearance that he had no home. We became fast friends immediately, especially after I shared my salami sandwich with him.

By the fourth night I found myself thinking more than usual about home. *Maybe my parents really want me after all* kept stealing into the back of my mind. *And I do sort of miss my sister and brothers—especially my sister, Carmen.*

When the sixth day arrived, I wanted to return home very badly, but I was also petrified. *They really hate me now for running away,* I assured myself. But the more I thought about it, the more I knew I couldn't stay away much longer.

Freedom to do as I pleased had been exciting, but my excruciating loneliness was a different matter and something I hadn't anticipated.

"Why doesn't anyone care about me?" I cried as I threw myself face down upon the ground. I wondered why God didn't care. *Or is there a God?* I began to question. "If there is a God," I shouted, "then why am I here alone? Why did I have to be born?"

After a time of wrestling with long-suppressed emotions, I wanted to throw myself into the river and drown. My family and the whole world would be better off without me. After wallowing in self-pity for a while, I picked myself up and, walking through a tobacco field, rolled some of the large leaves and smoked them. Immediately uncontrollable coughing and choking tore at my lungs, and my throat burned like a prairie fire.

By the seventh day I turned in the direction of home. Punishment or not, anything would be better than this unbearable world of silence and aloneness. Even the scraggly dog had abandoned me.

When finally I caught sight of the big house on the hill, panic seized me. *What will they do to me?* My heart beat wildly. Better wait until dark and then creep in unnoticed. The hours dragged, and it seemed the sun obstinately refused to slip behind the mountains. Never had I felt so alone, so isolated. Obsessed with fear, tortured with hatred and rebellion, I could hear the other children playing and their sounds of laughter filled the air. *No one cares about me,* I thought. I waited for what seemed an endless period of time, but at last the crimson clouds of sunset turned gray and night settled in. Cautiously I moved toward the top of the hill. I finally reached the broad veranda porch safely and crawled underneath its latticed floor to wait a few moments. Gathering all my courage, I crept out and darted up the six familiar steps, through the front door, and up the darkened stairway to my bed.

Though I was home, things were not the same. I refused to talk to anyone. Bitterness settled into my youthful spirit. I began to withdraw, fearful even to look into anyone's eyes. My parents ignored me, probably assuming I was going through a stage and it would pass in time. I was glad for their indifference. *They can't hurt me anymore if they don't love me and don't pay any attention to me.* But I was wrong. Too young to realize that the wounds inflicted by withholding love penetrated far deeper even than irresponsible punishment, I now began to have weird, obsessing thoughts—that I truly was the son of evil, that we all were, and that my brothers would soon turn against me. I became afraid of darkness and night, I alienated myself from everyone, lived in turmoil, and never expressed myself to a soul.

My course for future years was now set. Programmed for a life of rejection, bitterness, and loneliness, I began to build formidable walls to shut everyone out. *That way,* I subconsciously reasoned, *no one can hurt me anymore. If I'm rejected, I won't feel it.* But of course I was making a mistake. I was getting walled into loneliness.

Have you ever wondered how people get walled into loneliness? Every lonely person relates to walls and the feeling of being trapped in a prison. Knowing how it happened may help to tear down the walls. I would like to suggest a few ways we can slip into the prison of loneliness:

1. *Early childhood rejection.* Unfortunately, it happens whether we understand it or not. It helps if we can understand, but we're not trapped for life if we don't.

2. *Adverse circumstances.* Again, we can't always change our circumstances. At times we can, and we should in those instances. When we can't, we must learn how to make our situations work *for* us. What is that little prayer? "God, give us serenity to accept what cannot be changed, courage to change what should be changed, and wisdom to distinguish the one from the other."

3. *Oversensitiveness.* Many of us take life too seriously. We are just waiting for someone to slight us so we can say, "Aha. Just as I thought. He really doesn't like me." A sense of lightheartedness and humor are good qualities to develop. Learn to laugh. Even at yourself.

4. *Guilt.* Whether real or imagined, guilt isolates us and inflicts untold damage on our inner psyche, including loneliness. More will be said about this later in the book.

5. *An unfriendly spirit.* Those who always wait for others to speak first or to initiate friendship remain friendless. Force yourself, if necessary, to be the first to say "hello." Smile when you say it. Usually that's all you have to do to prompt a response.

As I look back on my life, I can see how the walls grew higher and accumulated more solid proportions, and I finally found myself in an unexpectedly helpless state. At first, I constructed those walls only to protect myself. It's true that they blocked the entrance to those whose rejection could inflict further wounds, but another thing happened that I was oblivious to. By the time I reached teenage years, I was trapped inside. No one could get in, and I couldn't get out. I sat there all alone, and my prison was as real as steel bars and concrete enclosures.

2

No Hope for Me Now

> Loneliness is undoubtedly the plague of those teen
> years. It is, in fact, a built-in risk as young people grow
> and begin to become individuals.[1]

It never occurred to me during my adolescent years to wonder if other teens were experiencing inward struggles similar
to mine. I knew my life was far removed from the norm, and
that the average young person was not involved in crime. I
was also too busy trying to impress my peers with a tough
exterior and, at the same time, trying to avoid probing
deeply enough to force a recognition of what really was going on inside. Yet the fact remains that my spiritually lost condition was the driving force behind my antisocial behavior.

So it is with most youth today whose hostile actions
plunge them on a collision course against constructive preparation for fulfillment in later years. With no understanding
of their inner conflict, no knowledge of how to resolve their
problems, and no particular reason to strive for loftier goals,
they choose irresponsible conduct, shrug their shoulders,
and excuse themselves with "everybody's doing it."

Whatever assumption is used, it all adds up to the same

thing—a blatant refusal to face the real issue, be it loneliness, insecurity due to rejection, feelings of inferiority, rebellion to established authority, or the absence of the love of God in Christ Jesus.

By the time I was sixteen, my parents gave up on me and sent me to New York to live with one of my brothers. Reviewing those former impressionable years at home in Puerto Rico, I recognize the fact that my early defiance in running away from authority at age nine became a pattern during the next six years. I had trouble at home. I had trouble at school. I wouldn't study, wouldn't let *anyone* push me around—whether parents, students, or teachers. I was always fighting, and when things got too tough, I took to the road. But there was no way I could move ahead academically. I was promoted from grade to grade, but only because the teachers couldn't endure another year of me. I didn't learn a thing.

I began to suspect that my mother realized her mistake of many years ago when I was but an impressionable child, but she never could bring herself to admit it. Fierce pride kept her silent. The intervening strife-filled years of severe punishment to divert my wayward tendencies only accelerated my father's determination to straighten me out, which, in turn, intensified my rebellion. Both Papa and I had terrible tempers, and because Mama was deathly afraid that he would kill me in one of his uncontrollable rages, her intervention only worsened matters.

When I ran away, the police usually found me and returned me to my parents, but I knew, and they knew, that I would leave again. One day I would run so far that no one could ever bring me back.

When it got to the place that I was gone as much as home, my parents knew they had to do something. "Finally, in desperation, Papa and Mama wrote my brother, Frank, asking him if he would let me come and live with him. Frank agreed, and plans were made for me to go."[2] Papa drove me to the airport in his old pickup truck after Mama tearfully hugged me, and the other children had waved their good-bys. When I turned from them slightly embarrassed, I walked toward the pickup without a backward glance. I would be free soon. Really free!

After the 45-minute drive to the San Juan airport, Papa handed me my ticket, stuck a folded $10 bill in my hand, and reminded me that Frank would be waiting at the airport in New York. His choked voice at the steps of the plane surprised me. I was even more surprised when he folded my frail body within his strong arms and whispered, "Hijo mio" (My son). "Be a good boy, little bird," he said as I ran up the steps of the plane and took my seat beside a window.

As the huge bird lifted off the runway, I pressed my face against the tiny window and watched the swaying palm trees grow smaller, the little island in the midst of the blue waters diminish and finally disappear. A great sense of detachment swept over me. All I had ever known—my whole life and context of familiarity—had slipped away, and I was swiftly moving into the vast unknown.

What was it Papa had called me, "Little bird"? My mind recaptured a rare occurrence of several years previous when we both sat on the steps of our large front porch and Papa told me a legendary story of the island about a little bird without legs who had to remain constantly in flight.

"He has no legs—no feet—he is forever moving," Papa said. "The only time he ever stops flying—the only time he comes to earth—is when he dies. Once he touches the earth, he can never fly again."

My youthful imagination tried to picture this pathetic little creature when Papa ended his story.

"That's you, Nicky," he spoke slowly. "You're restless. Like the little bird, you're always on the run."

Now the little bird was inside a great bird, caught up into space. As the hours passed, a feeling of bleakness and desolation deepened, and a pain that wouldn't leave stabbed at my chest. The farther we traveled, the greater the pain. I had a long time to think—to ponder my future.

Do I really want to live with my brother? I asked myself. I had never met my brother's wife, never seen his small child. In fact, I really didn't know Frank either. He had left home when I was very young, and it was almost as if I would be staying with a stranger.

No, I decided, *I want to be free. If that little bird dies when it stops flying, I'd better fly as long as I can. I don't want anyone, including my big brother, telling me what to do.*

When the plane landed in New York City, I wasn't prepared for the dramatic contrast to the balmy weather I had left behind. Dirty, slushy January snow covered the sidewalks and piled high alongside the buildings and at the corners. My thin tropical clothing was little defense against the icy winds and chilling cold. I had slipped away from the accompanying stewardess in the crowded airport so Frank wouldn't see me and take me to his apartment, and now I was darting in and out of building entrances as I wandered through the city. I finally found an old coat thrown across a garbage can in a back alley. The sleeves dropped over my hands and the hem scraped the sidewalk. Buttons were gone and pockets torn open, but so what? It kept me warm.

For three days I roamed the dirty, sloppy, unfriendly streets of New York—as lonely and lost as I'd ever been in my life. It never occurred to me that my almost nonexistent knowledge of the English language would prevent communication with my new world. No one seemed to notice me, much less care.

When I could stand the hunger no longer, I ventured into a little restaurant and ordered a hot dog by pointing to a picture of one. I gobbled it up and gestured that I wanted another one. The large man in a greasy, once white, apron standing in front of me shook his head sideways and held out his hand. I quickly searched my pocket and pulled out the $10 bill papa had given me at the airport. His big hand closed over it, he stuck it into his apron pocket, and brought me another hot dog and a bowl of chili. That was the last I ever saw of the man. Or my money.

I shuffled on down the street . . . moving . . . moving . . . always moving. If I stopped anywhere too long, the freezing temperatures penetrated to the marrow of my bones. I kept hoping someone would stop and ask if he could help me, but no one did. By midnight the third night, I began to fear that if I didn't get help soon, someone would find my frozen body on the sidewalk the next morning. I never knew a person could be so lonely in the midst of a million people.

Too weary to continue, I sat down on a curb to review my now hopeless situation. Bent over with my head resting on my arms, I could hear heavy, sloshing footsteps moving in my direction. It was a familiar sound. They would soon pass. But they didn't! They stopped right in front of me. Slowly I lifted my eyes to a big pair of dirty, wet, rubber boots connected to a blue uniform and ending with a policeman's cap. His face was not angry, and he didn't scowl.

"What're ya doin' sitting here in the middle of the night, kid?" he asked.

Laboriously I tried to explain in my broken English that I was lost. He seemed to know a few words in Spanish, so I showed him the slip of paper Mama had given me with Frank's name and phone number and said as clearly as I could, "Brother." I pointed and again said, "Brother."

He nodded, took my arm, lifted me to my feet, and walked to a phone booth. In a minute he handed me the phone, and I heard Frank's sleepy voice at the other end. Within an hour we were climbing up to Frank's third-floor apartment. Relieved and happy to see me, Frank greeted me enthusiastically and sat me down to a steaming bowl of soup.

Frank knew I had run away at the airport after he checked into the stewardess's report, so he was worried and fearful what to tell Papa. As for me, although the nightmare of being so lost and alone was over, I was not much happier at Frank's. I didn't belong there. I didn't want to be there, and I knew my stay would be brief.

I didn't make things easier, either. Frank had enrolled me immediately in the tenth grade of a school that was almost entirely black and Puerto Rican. It was run more like a reformatory than a public school, and the faculty spent the majority of their time trying to maintain discipline rather than teaching. It was a wild place of fights and immorality, and everyone was in a constant battle against those in authority. To survive, I became a part of the whole scene, venting my pent-up hatred in bloody fighting. After one particular classroom fight, when I knocked a kid unconscious with a chair, the principal warned me not to come back. I'd been in school two months when it happened, and I hadn't progressed academically in a single class. *What have I got to lose?* I asked myself. The answer was obvious. *Nothing.*

The next afternoon I left a note for Frank on the kitchen table telling him I wouldn't be back. I knew enough about the big city to find my way around.

The next three years witnessed my plummet from a mere rebellious teenager to a violent, hardened street-gang leader. The Mau Maus, the largest and toughest gang of hoodlums ever to roam the crime-infested streets of Brooklyn, became my domain.

For a while, maybe two years or so, I thought I had my little world in my hand. I had to act tough to protect my "macho" image—my manhood. I could not show fear, or even humanness, so I guzzled alcohol, proved myself in bed with girls, fought bloody fights, and vigorously maintained the facade.

Then one day I began to sense that I was living a double life. After I would say good-by to the gang, usually in the wee hours of morning, I began to feel the loss of the security of the group I left behind in order to return to my tiny room. I began to feel an agony coming on. Walking the dark, deserted streets on my way home, I dreaded the loneliness that awaited me. How I began to detest that dingy hole with its four ugly, paint-streaked walls and cracked ceiling! Even with its scarcity of beat-up furniture—only a bed and two chairs—it was crowded. Two windows and a sink completed the decor, and the floor was littered with cigarette butts and beer cans.

More often than I cared to admit, I lay awake at night staring at the ceiling. I struggled to fall asleep so I could escape from my incriminating thoughts, but sleep never came easily. All the ugliness and the violent events of the day kept reenacting themselves in my brain, and guilt throbbed within. Sometimes I would pound my fist or my head against the wall.

The man that I beat into a bloody pulp tonight—did he live? Does he have a wife? Children? The louder my conscience screamed, the more I had to drown it in alcohol, "grass," and pills. Everyone else was doing it, too.

In the morning, when at last out of sheer weariness I dropped off to sleep, Latin music blared out of open windows, mothers screamed at their children, and the smell of greasy food filled the air. Sirens, screams, fighting, cursing, loud music, lights flashing through windows—all made sleep impossible.

After a losing fight with the pillow, I rolled out of bed, dressed in a daze, and headed out for the streets. Looking around, I saw condemned buildings, filth, odors that turned my stomach, the unshaven faces of winos with eyes staring up out of the gutters, nearby garbage cans running over with humans and rats alike rummaging through them to find whatever food scraps were available. *Who wants to live in this hell hole?* I began to wonder. *But what choice do we have?*

Somehow, I knew I didn't belong in that confusion. I hated it. I hated the feeling of being alone, desolate, and sad. But hating it didn't change it. I had no power or ability to head down a different road. It was as if my course was set, and I couldn't veer to the left or to the right.

I had been picked up by the police many times so I was no stranger to them, or their jails, but they had never been able to hold me. No one would testify against me because they knew that when I got out I'd kill them, or the Mau Maus would do it for me.

One day after waiting in jail nearly a week for my hearing, I was handcuffed and marched into the courtroom. After routine questioning, the rather stern-faced judge with rimless glasses surprised me by saying, "Come up here, Nicky Cruz, and stand before the bench."

The judge leaned over and looked straight at me. He cleared his throat and began, "Nicky, I've got a boy just about your age. He doesn't get into trouble . . . like you . . . and the reason is because he has someone to love him. Obviously, you don't have anyone to love you—and you don't love anyone either. You don't have the capacity to love. You're sick, Nicky, and I want to know why. . . . I'm going to put you under the custody of our court psychologist, Dr. John Goodman. . . . He will examine you and make the final decision."[3]

In recalling those experiences of my life with the Mau Maus, it almost seems as if they happened in another lifetime. If I plunge too deeply into a self-incriminating recollection of specific incidents, I can still be overwhelmed with a sense of guilt. The apostle Paul warned us of this danger when he said, "Forgetting those things which are behind, and reaching forth unto those things which are before, I press toward the mark for the prize . . ." (Phil. 3:13–14).

Remembering the past, however, can be constructive, and we will take a moment to assess the positive aspects of a miserable adolescent history such as mine. In retrospect, these are some of the lessons I learned that prepared me for the next dramatic event in my life:

1. *Sin,* whether extreme in form such as I experienced, or simple, produces guilt, fear, shame, and eventually alienation from God and man. The trouble with even small sins is that they do not remain small. In a period of time we can become so entangled in the hopeless web of wrongdoing that we are afraid to face another day.

2. *Counting on people,* even friends, is a dead end. Our basic nature, which revolves around self, instinctively seeks self-preservation in any conflict of interest. The end result always deals disappointment to the one depending on the support of another.

3. *Loneliness* can be helpful, or, as one prominent youth leader of today expressed it, "Loneliness can be a friend" to drive us to God. I didn't realize it, of course, but my heart was being uniquely prepared for God by the realization of emptiness within.

4. *Love* is the key to loneliness and lostness. What was it the old judge said? Basically, he expressed the thought that the reason for my hopeless condition was that I had no one to love me. He was right. I didn't even know the meaning of the word. I may have acted blasé to the suggestion, but I knew he spoke the truth. What I didn't know was how to remedy my situation.

But God knew, and His timing and method would be perfect.

3

Touched by Love

Love is the key! So it is—and that's easy to say, but I suspect those words fall on lonely hearts in the same way they did mine. Yes, I needed someone to love me as a teenage hoodlum on the streets of New York. No, I couldn't love anyone until I felt securely loved myself. If I had been really loved and accepted for the person I was, chances are I would not have been so lonely. Beautiful hypothetical statements, but that's all they are to the thousands of lonely people in the world who see no hope for love in their lives.

For instance, the kids in the New York gangs ranging in age from twelve to eighteen are largely offspring of alcoholic parents, prostitutes, or economically depressed people who didn't want them in the first place. They entered the world unwanted. Early in life they sensed disapproval for reasons they couldn't understand, and the scars of their rejection grew deeper with every passing year. Who can love these misfits? Who wants to?

Only one prospect for hope exists in all the world for these people. Let me broaden the scope of our consideration. No matter how rejected or how loved by others a person might be, the loneliest condition known to humanity is that of being without God.

Yes, love is the key. The love of Jesus Christ, about which I knew nothing, was my only hope. But it took love in the heart of a fellow human being, who entered my darkened world and translated the message in words I could understand, to make that hope a reality.

It happened like this . . .

"Nicky, Jesus loves you."

Three times I had heard that ominous statement from a man we all called "the skinny preacher." I knew his real name. The first time I ever saw him at the school just across from my apartment he had walked over to me in front of a big crowd of gang members, stuck out his hand, and said, "Nicky, my name is David Wilkerson. I'm a preacher from Pennsylvania."

I just stared at him and said, "Go to hell, preacher."

Undaunted, this puny little weakling continued, "I've come to tell you about Jesus, Nicky. He really loves you."

"I felt like a trapped animal about to be caged. Behind me was the crowd. In front of me was the smiling face of this skinny man talking about love. No one loved me. No one ever had. As I stood there, my mind raced back to that time so many years ago when I heard my mother say, 'I don't love you, Nicky.' I thought, *if your own mother doesn't love you, then no one loves you—or ever will.*

"'You come near me, preacher, and I'll kill you,' I had said, shrinking back toward the protection of the crowd. I was afraid, and I didn't know how to deal with it."[1]

My second encounter was the same day, shortly after that first one. Scared, I had barged through the crowd, grabbed my girl-friend, Lydia, and headed up St. Edward Street away from the school. Once safely in the basement room where the Mau Maus hung out, I turned the record player on as loud as it would play and began to dance with

Lydia. Why couldn't I drown out the sound of those three stupid words, "Jesus loves you"?

Soon I sensed a disturbance at the door. Looking up, I saw this same skinny preacher standing at the entrance. In this filthy basement room he looked ridiculously out of place in his white shirt, neat suit, and tie.

"Where's Nicky?" he asked one of the boys.

Nodding his head toward me, Israel, my best friend, quickly walked away. Wilkerson stalked across the room as if he owned the place. A big smile on his face, he stuck out his hand again and said, "Nicky, I just wanted to shake hands with you. . . ."

Before he could finish, I slapped him in the face—hard. Then I spit on him.

"Nicky, they spit on Jesus, too," this now obnoxious-to-me person persisted.

"Get the hell out of here!" I shouted, and pushed him backward toward the door.

"Before I leave, Nicky, I just want to tell you again. Jesus loves you."

"Get out, you crazy priest. You don't know what you're talking about." Now I was screaming at the top of my lungs. "I'll give you twenty-four hours to get off my turf or I'll kill you!"

Backing out the door, still smiling, he calmly repeated, "Remember, Nicky, Jesus loves you."

Didn't this lunatic know I *really could* kill him? It wouldn't be the first time I killed someone. I reached down and picked up an empty wine bottle and smashed it to the floor. I had never felt so frustrated, so desperate, so completely helpless in my life.

All the other guys knew that this Wilkerson had really gotten under my skin. There was only one way to fool them, and that was to act tough. I didn't want to lose the respect of my gang.

"That stupid, crazy witch," I fumed. "If he comes back

here, I'll set him on fire." I slammed the door behind me and stood on the sidewalk looking after him as he walked away. *He ain't gonna scare me,* I thought. *Nobody's gonna scare me.* But all I could hear in my mind was the voice of that skinny preacher saying over and over, "Nicky, Jesus loves you."

Encounter number three took place early the next morning. All night long I had tossed and turned and stared at the ceiling. I smoked one cigarette after another. I couldn't rest. I couldn't sleep. I did everything to silence that voice, but the words echoed in my brain throughout the night. "Nicky, Jesus loves you. Jesus loves you. . . ."

Finally, I turned on the light and looked at my watch —5:00 A.M. No use wrestling with the pillow any longer. I got up, dressed, picked up my cigarettes, walked down the three flights of stairs, and opened the front door of the building. "The sky was just beginning to turn gray. In the distance I could hear the sounds of the great city as it yawned and stretched to life.

"I sat on the front steps with my head in my hands. *Jesus loves you . . . Jesus loves you . . . Jesus loves you.*"[2]

A car pulled up and a door slammed shut. When I lifted my weary head and focused bloodshot eyes, the same skinny preacher was standing in front of me. Placing his hand on my shoulder, again smiling, he said, "Hi, Nicky! Remember what I told you last night? I just wanted to come by and tell you once more that Jesus loves you."

I'd had enough. Jumping to my feet, I took a swing at him. He moved back out of reach, and as I stood there glaring at him like an animal ready to leap, "Wilkerson looked me straight in the eye and said, 'You could kill me, Nicky. You could cut me in a thousand pieces and lay them out on the street. But every piece would cry out, Jesus loves you . . .'"[3]

Drained of every defense, I just stood there and stared at him.

"You're afraid, aren't you, Nicky? You're sick of your sin and you're *lonely.*" He spoke quietly, but with great strength and conviction. "But Jesus still loves you," he added.

How did he know that I was lonely? I hardly knew it myself. When he spoke of sin, I hadn't known what he was talking about and I was afraid to admit my fear. "But how did he know I was lonely? The gang was always with me. I had any of the girls I wanted. People were afraid of me—they would see me coming and move off the sidewalk and into the street. I had been the leader of the gang. How could anyone think I was lonely? And yet, I was. And now this preacher knew it."[4]

"You think you're going to change me just like that?" I said, snapping my fingers.

Ignoring my insolent remark, he continued as if there had been no interruption. "Nicky, you didn't sleep much last night, did you?"

Stunned, I wondered how he knew this. "To tell you the truth, I didn't sleep much last night either," Wilkerson continued. "I stayed awake most of the night praying for you. And I want to tell you again, Nicky, that someone really cares for you. Jesus does." He paused several moments, then added with a look of certainty and a tone of authority, "One day soon, Nicky, God's Spirit is going to deal with you, and you are going to stop running away and come running to Him."

In the deep of my heart I knew he spoke the truth. I also knew I would fight to the bitter end. I couldn't help myself. I had been a fighter too long just to roll over and give up.

Without saying a word I stood up, turned my back to him, and walked into the trash-littered building, shutting the door behind me. Climbing up the steps to my room, I sat on my bed and looked out the window. It was still early morning, the gray had turned crimson, and I knew instinctively that the end of my running was close.

Is there really something more to life than this? Can anything—or anyone—drown out this unutterable loneliness? Deeper and deeper I probed, but there were no answers inside of me. Outwardly, I went through all the motions of life as usual. But I knew nothing was usual, or ever would be again.

Two weeks passed, and although I had not seen Wilkerson again, his piercing words continued to chip away at my closed heart. I began to suspect that Israel, my best friend in the gang, was secretly seeing that detested preacher. He kept bugging me about him. Every time I saw Israel, he said something about God.

"'Damn it, Israel, if you don't shut up about that God stuff, I'm gonna kill you,'"[5] I lashed out at him one day.

But Israel didn't shut up. He kept talking about it, and I didn't like it. Even though I was miserable on my one-way road to hell, I was afraid of what Wilkerson represented. At least I was familiar with my road. The unknown terrified me.

About the middle of that scorching summer, Israel came by and told me about a big meeting Wilkerson was having over at St. Nicholas Arena. In fact, Wilkerson had been talking to Israel and had issued a personal invitation to the Mau Maus. He was sending a bus to pick us up and would reserve a special section up front in the big auditorium.

"I'm not going," I shrugged, then turned and walked away. "You guys can go, but I'm not."

"Whatsa matter, Nicky?" Israel called. "You chicken? That's it! You're chicken."

Israel touched my most vulnerable spot. "I'm not afraid of no one. *No one,* you hear?" I shouted. "Not you, not that skinny preacher . . . not even God." That settled it.

Israel just stood there. "Sounds to me like you're scared of something. How come you won't go?"

If I didn't go in the face of Israel's challenge, they'd all think I was scared. I knew I didn't have a choice. "Yeah, well, I'll show you guys I ain't scared o' nothin'. I'll be on that bus."

I was. When we piled off the bus, we stormed into that arena past two ushers who tried to stop us at the door. Israel and I led the parade as everyone turned around to see what the commotion was. We were "on stage" and we made the most of it.

Bedlam soon broke loose in that crowd. The arena was almost full, and as I looked around, I could see members of rival gangs all over the place. A full-scale rumble could be in the making. One thing was certain—I would do my best to promote it.

When the organ started to play, several of the fellas and girls close to the front leaped up on the stage and began to perform—girls shaking their hips double-beat to the music, and the boys jitterbugging around them. Wild applause, whistles, and shouts of approval filled the place. Things were beginning to get out of hand.

Just then a girl walked onto the center of the stage and stood behind the microphone waiting for the noise to subside. It grew louder. The girl began to sing anyway, even though it was impossible to hear her. She finished her song and walked nervously off the stage.

Now Wilkerson appeared and stepped to the microphone. A momentary lull of expectancy swept over the crowd, and he swiftly took advantage of it and began to speak: "Tonight I'm going to ask my friends, the Mau Maus, to receive the offering."

I couldn't believe my ears. He would trust *us,* knowing the reputation we had with money! The audience began to laugh aloud and applaud. This was going to be the biggest joke of all.

Jumping to my feet, I pointed to some of the guys. "Let's go!" I motioned. Six of us climbed the steps and lined up across the front of the stage. A large ice-cream carton was handed to each of us while Wilkerson instructed us to stand in front of the platform while people came forward to give their offering. "When it's finished, come around behind that curtain" he pointed, "and onto the stage. I'll be waiting for you to bring me the offering."

My first impulse was to take the money and disappear behind those curtains. Those would be the easiest bucks we'd ever come by, and besides, everyone was expecting us to do that. However, a strange feeling began to come over me as people streamed up the aisles and dropped their offering, money they didn't *have* to give, into the cartons. I couldn't remember ever being trusted with anything in all my life. Not even as a small child. Someone had confidence in me now, and that trust ignited a spark inside. As the spark grew warmer, it touched my heart, and I felt good about myself for the first time in years. I liked the feeling.

It was even better when I marched up to the stage and handed the money to Wilkerson. "Thank you, Nicky. I knew I could count on you." Wilkerson smiled as he took the carton from me. Choosing right instead of wrong seemed to have its own reward. I was astonished.

Wilkerson began to preach. At first I couldn't hear what he was saying. I was too caught up with the glowing feeling inside of me that seemed to be spreading, and the newness of this experience completely absorbed my attention for a while.

Suddenly, however, I began to hear. When Wilkerson first told me that Jesus loved me, I really didn't know who Jesus was. Now he was telling the story of Jesus Christ, His total life, what really happened. This was the first time I had ever heard that story—where He came from, what He did, the healing of the sick, restoring sight to the blind, feeding the multitudes, His rejection, how His enemies paid a gang to go after Him, His crucifixion. I was captivated! I began to relive the life of Jesus, hardly conscious that there was anyone else in that auditorium but Jesus and me. How I hated those skunks that betrayed and killed Him! I wanted to fight for Jesus Christ, kill those tormentors.

For the first time I fully realized that *I* deserved death, but *He* deserved life. He was pure, honest, truth—and I was a liar, no good, cast out, a filthy underdog. The Holy Spirit began a tremendous momentum within, and the whole atmosphere was charged with a power I couldn't withstand.

Then I heard a voice, as if from some other world, saying that the Mau Maus were ready to fight. "Cool it," I scowled. "No one's going to fight right now." After a moment it was as if there was someone else inside of me who added: "This man is right. I don't understand it, but we're going to sit here and listen." Everyone settled down again.

I looked around, and it was as if the glory of the Lord began to overpower the whole atmosphere. St. Nicholas Arena was an auditorium used mainly for wrestling and boxing matches, but now it seemed as though God had walked right in with all His angels and taken control, casting out the evil forces residing in that place. You could see Christians beginning to unite, heads were bowing in prayer, and hands were reaching out for other hands. As the Holy Spirit obviously moved, much interceding began for David Wilkerson. He was searching for words, broken, sensitive.

"He is here, He is here," he was saying. And every person in that huge arena knew it. He had been talking about the love of God in sending His Son to die for us. "We complain so loudly at the least little thing anyone does to us that's wrong," he asserted. "Think of Jesus. He never did anything wrong to anyone, yet He took a crown of thorns on His head, carried a heavy cross on His back. He could have called ten thousand angels to rescue Him if He had wanted to. The only time He opened His mouth after they nailed Him to that cross was to forgive a thief beside Him who deserved to die. 'Today you will be with me in Paradise,' He told that guilty robber. Jesus was broken in His body, yet His dying concern was for us."

A more powerful force was operating inside of me than I had ever known, and I seemed helplessly swept along by a tide I couldn't resist. I had no control over my emotions, my actions, my thoughts, or even my words. I had no idea what was going on inside of me.

Then I heard Wilkerson say something about repenting for sin. At that moment, a review of my whole life began parading before my eyes. I almost felt detached from the scenes flashing before me, and yet I knew I wasn't. I closed my eyes as I saw the lies I had told, the hurt I had inflicted on others, things I had stolen, the bloody fights, the stabbings, the girls, lust, sex, the hatred for my parents. My parents! *How painful is this human life when you don't have purpose for living,* I thought. In that moment I groped to understand why my mother had so destroyed me with hatred. Then I began to realize that all this time I had been wrong, the image I had portrayed before everyone was false—and it "blew my mind."

I heard people all around me crying, and beside me Israel was loudly blowing his nose. Something mysterious indeed was happening in that place. Wilkerson said with a new tone of authority, "Those who will receive Jesus Christ and be changed, stand up and come forward."

Instantly Israel jumped to his feet and announced, "Boys, I'm going up. Who's going with me?" Twenty-five or thirty Mau Maus responded.

"Come on, Nicky," he pleaded with me as I remained seated.

Shaking my head negatively, I said, "No." Israel persisted, and finally I got up and moved down the aisle with the others.

When we arrived at the front, tears streamed down Israel's face as he told Wilkerson, "I want you to pray for me. I want Christ in my life." Soon Wilkerson dismissed the service and took us to a basement room for counseling.

While Wilkerson prayed for the whole group, I watched him with open eyes. I felt his sincerity, his compassion, his tenderness. It was obvious that he was really in love with

Jesus Christ, and that the love of Jesus was reaching out to us. There was nothing phony about this guy.

"Nicky, I've been praying for you day and night for two weeks," Wilkerson said to me at length. "Now, let me pray with you. Jesus is willing to help you, to take away your loneliness, to live inside of you, build a new kingdom inside, make you strong, make you love yourself, and even make you love your enemies."

That was too heavy for me. I felt like crying, but instead I bit my lips so the pain would keep me from responding. Deliberately I turned around to walk out, but in that moment the Holy Spirit completely overpowered me. Fifteen or sixteen of those tough, vicious guys, whom I had never seen in a weak moment, were falling on their knees and crying. I looked over at Carlos—that bloodthirsty, insensitive, vicious fighter who never had sympathy for anyone—and he was crying and calling, "Jesus, Jesus, Jesus." Then I glanced over at Israel, who seemed drowning in his own tears. I said to my best friend, "What the hell is wrong with you?"

"I just gave my whole life to Jesus, Nicky, and I don't feel lonely anymore," Israel said with a shining face. "I feel so good, Nicky."

I began to feel envious. "I don't feel lonely anymore," Israel had said. The weight of my own loneliness began to bear down heavily on me, and a tremendous force laid hold of me. All of a sudden I fell to my knees and began crying. I had not cried since I was eight years old, but now the dam broke, the floodgates opened, and the tears literally poured down my cheeks. My heart felt punished by enormous loads of guilt, and I felt ashamed, embarrassed, crushed. I covered my face so no one could see me cry, but the tears ran down between my fingers, washing both my face and hands. My chest ached so badly that I could hardly breathe. I felt unworthy. As I sobbed, I felt my whole world collapse, but at the same time I knew it was being put back together in a new way. Restored. It was as if I had been wheeled into the operating room, laid out on a table, put to sleep, and Jesus cut open my chest, took my old heart out, and put a new one back in. The most tremendous peace I ever experienced filled that new heart, and though the day was hot and muggy, cool water seemed to pour over me and I felt refreshed.

Healing took place in my mind. Instantly all the memories of my past were cleansed and I felt as if I had just been born from my mother's womb all over again. I cried aloud, "I don't know who You are, Jesus Christ. You say You love me. Do You love me? Do You *really* love me? Oh, God, I don't even believe in love. I don't know what love is. Are You love? I'm so confused, but I know You are really here. I don't know what to do or say. All I can tell You is will You please help me, forgive me—oh, forgive me."

Then I felt Him saying within, "Yes, Nicky, I really do love you." Right there He filled me with forgiveness and love I had never known. I felt so good I started laughing and crying all at the same time. Some of the guys ran over and hugged me.

Finally I went up to the preacher, hugged him, and told him I knew Jesus loved me because I could feel Him in my heart.

"Oh, Nicky!" David exclaimed. "This is heaven, this is the kingdom of God. You're never going to walk alone again, never going to hurt alone again. God is your heavenly Father, and He will be with you through every storm, every doubt, every fear, every insecurity—everything. He is going to be there."

As I look back now on David Wilkerson's "love blitz," I see the following principles at work:

1. God is the source of love. The *only* source. If we are looking elsewhere, we'll never find it.

2. Regardless of our background, God's love and forgiveness are available to us all.

3. Sin in our lives must be confessed and forgiven by

God before we can know His love. When we sincerely repent, He always forgives.

4. Everyone, no matter how sinful, becomes a new person when forgiven by God and washed clean by Jesus Christ.

Before I left St. Nicholas Arena that night so many years ago, David Wilkerson gave me a Bible—a big one, that felt to me as if it weighed twenty-five pounds. When I walked out into the street I was a brand new person, with Jesus in my heart and a big, black Bible in my arms.

4

Young Only Once

No matter how many years separate me from that meeting in St. Nicholas Arena, the experience of receiving Jesus Christ as my Savior remains as fresh as if it happened last night. I remember every detail of the life-changing incident, and tears still dampen my eyes as I consider the depths to which Jesus reached in order to rescue me. The love that encompassed and filled me that night still drives me to other lost and lonely young people. I deeply relate to them, and when they say, "I'm so lonely I could die," I hear them. Loud and clear I hear them.

It may appear to others that these young people have no reason in the world to be lonely, but I know how they feel. I was there too long, and I suffered that pain too keenly to dismiss their cry. For example, the following letter is typical of the plight of many youth today:

Dear Nicky,

I am a sixteen-year-old girl. Things have really been depressing lately, and I'm a wreck inside. I am getting along with very few people. I just can't seem to make or keep friends. Life is such a hassle. I keep making the same mistakes over and over again.

I'm seeing a psychiatrist every two weeks, but I'm ready to commit myself someplace for good. I'm fed up with life. I'm a very lonely and confused person. I really want to be normal, but it's impossible for me.

I'm getting used by guys. All they want me for is sex. I've been pregnant eight times, but I've had miscarriages each time. I keep searching for answers, but I find nothing. I feel like hiding from everyone.

I struggle against depression and loneliness all alone. I never know who to really trust. I hate the way I look, and I hate the way my life is going. I hate my past, and I hate all the things I do wrong. I never really know which way to turn. Nicky, will you please, please pray for me and try to help me in some way.

I travel the world over holding crusades largely attended by the youth of every nation, and after these meetings I receive scores of letters like this one. Though the circumstances vary, the basic plea is the same. The youth of today are eating their hearts out with loneliness, meaninglessness, and hopelessness. Consider a paragraph from another letter:

Nicky, I was wondering if anyone can pull out of their loneliness? I don't want to live much longer like this if my life can't change. I feel as if no one really loves me. I think this letter is just about my last resort. I am hoping so much that you can help me. I really don't know what I'm expecting, but you seem such a great person, and I think you would be the only one in the world who could possibly even start to help me. I am begging you—please!!!

Can you imagine the heavy responsibility I carry day after day as I seek to minister life to hundreds of dying young people? Only the Holy Spirit within me can reach out to them and give them hope where there is no hope. I was a young person in the fifties and early sixties, so I can see clearly what is happening. The hurt, pain, and loneliness of the kids I grew up with on the streets of New York was only a fraction of what was yet to come. I knew then that young people were on a suicide trip, a collision course with life's harsh realities, ready to rock the very foundations of society. What began as just a small stream of mixed-up kids like myself has grown into an angry, roaring river heading straight for a plunging waterfall, and it looks as if nothing can divert them from total destruction. The tragedy is that the powerful undertow has sucked in almost all of today's youth. That's why I have dedicated my life to working with these angry, troubled, confused young people.

Though there were many contributing factors or persons that aided the rise of the youth movement, no person stands out more clearly than Elvis Presley. It was not just his influence on young people, but because he was a symbol of a new awakening among them. Until Elvis, all the emphasis in America was on adults. Society was geared to the mature generation. Then Elvis came along and insisted that young people had something important to say.

Through his music, his lifestyle, and his attitude, Elvis Presley brought a new spirit of independence. The whole nation turned around, and all the emphasis was focused away from the old to the young. Elvis was more important to America's youth than President Eisenhower, and the average young person received more attention than did adults.

The *record industry* was the first to change and become geared to the teenager. Then came *radio* and all the commercial market as advertising aimed at youthful consumers. Even General Motors, the largest corporation in the world, designed its *automobiles* for a sporty youth market demanding not a family sedan, but a fun machine. *Businesses, schools, churches,* and *families* all catered to the young.

Along with the emphasis on youth came the emphasis

on fun. Pleasure and entertainment was the name of the game. That's what life was all about. Even the new medium of *television,* which did so much to revolutionize society with its flow of facts, fantasy, amusement, and escape, merely added to the fun revolution.

America was at peace, World War II and the Korean conflict were far behind, and the economy was good. Young people felt that life was not that serious, and it was time to "Come On, Baby, Let the Good Times Roll—We're Gonna Rock Around the Clock." And they did.

Like an epidemic, the youth infection spread to Europe. It began with four scrawny Liverpool musicians named the Beatles. What started as a flickering flame in America ignited into an uncontrollable forest fire spread all over the world by the Beatles.

It was fun while it lasted, but like everything else in this harsh world, it had to end. The end came in the form of the Vietnam war for America, and economic chaos and communism for Europe. Now that young people seemed clearly in control, they didn't know how to handle disaster when it struck.

Their first reaction was to strike back at the older generation, causing the "generation gap." Soon they became smarter and decided to storm the "Establishment," taking control of government and wealth, as well as culture. To them the only way to handle things was to bring about political and social change as vast and as reckless as the cultural change initiated some ten years earlier.

The sobering sixties followed the fun-filled fifties. With the threat of nuclear war, racial injustices, Vietnam, governments collapsing all over the world, and three major assassinations in America, young people *suddenly took life very seriously.* They tried to change the system, but it didn't work. Nothing much was changed. There were lots of sparks, but no fire.

Rock festivals, which were supposed to usher in a new

era of peace and love, exploded into scenes of riot and brutal murders. The drug visions were beautiful for a while, but soon became nightmares of widespread drug deaths. Political protests turned into the hellish reality of four student deaths at Kent State University. When the flame of revolution died, and the smoke cleared away, nothing much had changed. The Establishment was still as big and as strong as ever.

Then Richard Nixon, a political conservative, won by a landslide over a liberal candidate in 1972, and it was obvious that the revolution had backfired. *But the world moved on.* Our youth were left in disillusionment without a cause to fight for or hope to live for. And if the failure of the youth political movements didn't strike the final blow to the dreams and aspirations of the young people, the Watergate scandal smashed them once and for all.

Their dreams were dashed. Their hope was gone. Their heroes were all dead. Young people today are desperately grasping for meaning to life, but it has eluded them. The youth of today may be wiser, but they are also much sadder. They realize at eighteen what it used to take until eighty to discover—there is no real hope to this life.

The political systems have failed, our leaders have failed, and young people cannot change themselves in this lost and dying world. What are the effects? For one thing, suicides in epidemic proportions are sweeping the youth scene.

"Although some suicides are drug-induced or impulsive acts," one authority has written, "most youthful suicides or attempted suicides have a history of unhappiness, fears, or loneliness behind them. Those who look to suicide as a solution already feel alone in this world, so they are able to rationalize their way out of it into the unknown."[1]

Young people are wallowing in a pit of hopelessness, and the tragedy of lost, lonely, confused, and angry youth all over the world faces us today. The saddest part of it all is that there are so many who feel there is *no answer.*

Answers are hard to produce, I have to admit, for many of today's youth are innocent victims at the hands of irresponsible adults. For instance, *child abuse* and *incest* are running rampant. Many people find it easier to ignore these abhorrently repulsive present-day realities, but in my many dealings with the youth culture, I cannot.

When I spoke at a crusade in Lausanne, Switzerland, in an auditorium constructed to seat 3500, but into which were jammed 4700, I felt the power of God heavily on me as I gave my testimony. My interpreter, a Frenchman, was one of the best I'd ever had. I could tell he was with me in spirit. It was one of those times when my vast audience was in the palm of my hand. They laughed when I said something funny, they grew solemn and hushed when I became serious. And 80 percent of that audience were young people.

After the message, many of those present received Jesus as their Savior. I stayed until very late speaking with as many as I could. Knowing I had to leave early in the morning for a crusade the next day in Germany, I gathered up my Bible and other belongings to head for the hotel.

As I walked out of the entrance into the cold March night, a young girl stood in the dim light smoking a cigarette and waiting for me.

"Could I please talk to you?" she asked in a matter-of-fact manner.

"I'd love to listen but I'm so tired. I need to go to the hotel and rest," I answered wearily. I started to walk away when she grasped my arm and pleadingly said, "I know you want to leave, but I need so much help, and God knows this is my last chance. I'm so confused I don't know what to do." She spoke perfect English.

I looked into her frantic eyes. Hadn't I committed my life, weary or not, to confused young people just like this girl standing in front of me? "What do you mean?" I responded. "Come on inside so I can talk to you."

"I can't leave this cigarette." The girl stood motionless.

"Come on in. I don't want to catch a cold," I insisted as I turned and walked inside.

When we moved in, she threw the cigarette on the floor and stepped on it. I collapsed into the nearest seat at the back of the still-lighted auditorium, and motioned for her to sit beside me.

"Tell me now what's troubling you," I said warmly.

"My name is Marie. I read your book and was very impressed and touched," she began. "As I was listening to you tonight, I kept thinking—Oh, God, he made it. He made it. But I'm too confused."

"What do you mean you are confused? In what way?" I probed.

"I'm very lonely, Nicky, and loneliness has made me do many ugly things, things that have left emotional scars I fear can never be healed," she said.

"Are you aware that in your loneliness there is Someone who can fill that void?" I answered, hoping to help the girl quickly so that I might get a little rest.

"I've taken too many drugs when I am depressed—too many uppers," she continued, almost as if she had not heard what I said. "I did have an experience with Christ when I was very young, just a little girl. But something terrible happened in my home. I know I have to tell you about it."

"Go on, Marie," I urged.

"You see, I developed physically very early. When I was only thirteen, I was aware that my father kept looking at me in a different way, but I was too young to understand. One day when my mother wasn't home, my father asked me to sit down with him. He started to kiss me, but I still didn't realize what he was doing. He got up, and soon I was aware that someone was behind me. When I glanced back, I saw that it was my father—and he was naked. He told me not to be afraid and began to kiss me again. Now I was scared to death. He began to take off my clothes, and since it was my father, I couldn't say anything. I closed my eyes, because in my innocent stupidity, I thought he was going to kill me. Suddenly he forced himself all over me, and I began to feel terrible pain. It hurt so much I thought I'd die. I was scared to tell my mama, so I ran away from home. They don't know where I am. Because of what happened, I lost all respect for my body, and now I give my body to anyone who wants it so I won't feel it was only my father." She looked at me with a dull, hopeless expression. "Nicky, I'm dying. I'm dead, and I'm only eighteen years old. I am running scared. I smoke too much, I'm high on drugs right now, I am corrupt, and I have VD, too."

As I looked at this blond, beautiful young girl, I was aghast. She was only eighteen, but I would have guessed her to be ten years older. My emotions within were so deep I couldn't speak. In that moment I felt an ugly, bitter spirit gripping me—anger for her father, hatred for the evil that was destroying her soul, compassion and an aching heart for this precious girl. I couldn't believe that a father—a professing Christian, Marie had told me—could care so little for his daughter that he would ruin her entire life to satisfy a moment of uncontrollable passion.

"I can't cry," she said, breaking the silence.

"How long has it been since you have cried?" I asked, realizing she had just thrown me an important key to unlocking her emotions.

"Since I was thirteen years old and ran away from home," she answered.

When I looked at her again, I thought of my own little daughters whose lives were so important to me, for whom I would die if need be, and I felt such deep anguish that hot tears of grief began streaming down my face.

"Regardless of what has happened," I said in a choked voice, "you must ask forgiveness for your father and yourself. You must go home."

Since there were a few Christian brothers left in the auditorium straightening chairs and puttings things away, I called them to come and pray with me. Putting my hands on the back of her head, I began to sob. My insides felt raw and bleeding for all the hurt this girl had borne. "Oh, God," I cried, "please touch Marie. Come and invade this broken, lonely life, this child of Yours who is dying of loneliness. Shadow of death, get out of her life. God, please resurrect her emotions."

As I prayed, I felt her body begin to shake. She was crying at last. I continued to pray. "Oh, God, restore her soul. You love her, and there is much healing needed here. Please begin right now. Fill her with Your life, and Your Spirit, and Your Word, and heal her."

She was on the floor sobbing now, her face covered by her hands. Then I heard her voice. "Oh, God," she wept, "thank You for making me cry. Thank You for helping me to feel again. Thank You for my sweet mother who loves You. Don't ever let her find out what happened with my father. And dear God, bring my father to Yourself. Help me to love him. Oh, I want to help others who are suffering like I am. Help me to let You be the Friend I need in my loneliness."

When her prayer was over and her convulsive weeping hushed, she got up and threw her arms around me. I looked once more into that face, and I couldn't believe what I saw. She was eighteen years old again with the freshness of youth sparkling from her eyes.

Today Marie is with an American family and is planning to move to the United States. God answered her prayer fully. Not only is she a healed, new person, but she is touching and helping other broken lives.

The world is filled with pathetic children like Marie. The ugliness of the sins of selfish adults visited on helpless children is a problem beyond solving. It flourished for years behind closed doors and closed mouths, but suddenly those mouths are open, and the world is hearing. But the world can't solve the mounting problem. All it can do is produce

TV documentaries, hold seminars, and try to reach and educate both abusive parent and abused child. The problem, however, is racing ahead of the cure.

As if incestuous fathers with daughters is not inconceivable enough, we now are learning that the latest assault on children is by mothers seducing sons. Unthinkable as it seems, this latest evil trend threatens to sweep the land, spawned by explicit movies and novels, with printed reviews of both. Fathers molesting daughters, we say, is one thing —but mothers? Preposterous! Yes, it is preposterous, but it's happening enough to receive media attention, and I predict that unless the hand of God intervenes, the tide of this evil will creep up into the shores of every corner of our world and further infect and pollute our priceless future heritage—children and youth.

Have I painted a hopeless picture? Can nothing be done to reverse youth's dilemma? Are there no answers?

There is *one* answer, only one! If I did not believe in that one answer, I wouldn't leave my home and family, exhausting myself to seek out troubled youth and give them that answer. JESUS CHRIST is the answer. Only He can scrape up the torn, scattered pieces of these wrecked lives, restore wholeness, and breathe new meaning and new hope into them. "For he has rescued us from the dominion of darkness and brought us into the kingdom of the Son he loves, in whom we have . . . the forgiveness of sins" (Col. 1:13 NIV).

Only Jesus Christ is the source of any hope, the source of any moral values, the source of any meaning to life. Only He can fill the lonely void in our hearts. "The heart is a lonely hunter," one has phrased it. And it's true.

Let's face it! Everyone is lonely sometime. If we're not careful, it's easy to miss our root problem and turn to drugs, alcohol, sex, materialism, or whatever is handy, never dealing with the basis of our need. Let's deal with loneliness, accept it, and make it work *for* us, not *against* us.

Since we've considered only one side of the youth picture, let's turn a page and look at the other side. It's true that Jesus Christ is the answer for the teenager whose life is broken and twisted from sin, but He is also the answer for those who choose another way. Two young people whom I've had opportunity to observe over a long period of time come to mind.

One of them, a seventeen-year-old girl who gave her life to Jesus Christ at an early age, decided that the path of obedience was the one for her. Of course, she experienced loneliness. She knew she would when she made her choice, but she has accepted the fact that loneliness is not the worst problem in the world. Even at seventeen, she knows that everything she compromises, in the long run, she is going to lose.

In spite of her unpopular choice, she is a cheerleader at her high school. Although it hurts me to see all the other cheerleaders heading for the wild, after-game parties while this young girl goes home, yet at the same time, I am proud.

One of my proudest moments came when a friend from North Carolina resented the strictness of this girl's parents, and she sweetly replied: "I'm going to listen to my daddy. He knows, because he's been there, and he deals with all kinds of kids." You see, *I* am that daddy, and Alicia, my firstborn, is that seventeen-year-old girl. I have told Alicia often that when you stand for the principle that you belong to Jesus Christ, that's when you know who you really are. I see a maturity in Alicia that is beyond her years. She knows who she is and where she is going.

David Harris is another example. A seminary student, he is one of the happiest young men I've ever known. He gave his life to Jesus Christ as a sophomore in high school, but he didn't give just part of it—he gave all of it. Because of his stand, David has known what it is to be lonely. He often knows what it is to be without close friends. He also knows that Jesus Christ can fill the lonely void and be the Friend he needs.

I am in constant touch with youth's culture, and in spite of the gloomy outlook on the youth scene, I am excited to report that there is a new and growing revolution. I hear the distant drums, and I see its troops steadily moving across the horizon. They are following a victorious leader, and they are gaining in strength and numbers. This is the revolution of change in Jesus Christ. The youthful Alicias and Davids are marching across our land in a counterrevolution. Their lives are not shattered by drugs, disillusioned by promiscuity, or deadened with alcohol. They are proving that Jesus Christ is, indeed, the answer. God give them courage!

Now let's consider a few personal involvement principles so that you may begin to understand the nature of the loneliness problem and head down the road to wholeness and healing:

1. If you have not received Jesus Christ as your personal Savior, or if you are unsure whether you have (religion, church attendance, baptism, or any other pious activity have no bearing upon this decision), do so at once. Simply come to God in prayer, ask Him to forgive your sins, and invite Jesus Christ into your heart. The Bible says, "But as many as received him [Jesus Christ], to all who believed in his name, he gave the right to become the children of God" (John 1:12).

2. Now pray about your loneliness. Tell God about it, and transfer your heavy load into His hands by an act of simple trust. Expect Him to help you. The Bible assures you that He will: "Casting all your care upon him; for he cares for you" (1 Peter 5:7).

3. Begin to look at loneliness in a positive way. Make it work *for* you, not against you. If you need to forgive, do it. If you need to confess the sin of self-pity, which almost always accompanies the feeling of loneliness, do it (1 John 1:9).

4. Begin a daily, disciplined quiet time of reading the Bible and praying. You will never become spiritually strong

enough to overcome loneliness or any other problem without receiving daily strength from God.

That's what happened to me after God's love was revealed to me. I experienced the truth of verses such as, "Now ye are clean through the word which I have spoken unto you" (John 15:3), and "Ask, and ye shall receive" (John 16:24). God does exactly what He promises, and you might as well begin taking Him at His word right now.

5

Success Is No Guarantee

Mountain climbers say it often: "The higher up you go, the lonelier it gets." The same experience applies to leaders who, in their climb to the top, have found that the oxygen gets thin, the available companionship increasingly sparse. The plains and mountains and valleys of human intercourse where a man or woman must maintain some vestige of the general can provide territory for acute isolation and loneliness.[1]

We are living in a day of emphasis on getting to the top. "See You At the Top," the title of a popular, fast-selling motivational book, is the battle cry of our modern society. We cannot rest or "stop to smell the flowers along the road," as the poet phrased it. If we do, someone else might inch ahead.

Somehow we imagine that the end of all problems awaits us at the magical summit of success, so we keep on climbing. We hear our families calling, and we look down to see them pleading with us to take a moment of relaxation with them. But there isn't time. *Don't they realize this sacrifice is for them? They simply will have to wait until I've got it made—then I'll have time for them.*

Everything is laid on the altar of reaching that pinnacle. Family, friends, health, recreation, and, yes—God. Especially God. On the way up, such sacrifices seem worth it all. *When I get up there,* we rationalize, *everyone will applaud.* People will be standing in line to be friends. Then I'll have time for all the things I've missed.

The tragedy is that it doesn't happen that way. Albert Einstein once wrote to a friend, "It is strange to be known so universally and yet to be so lonely."

Albert Einstein was not alone. Few who have attained nobility in any field of endeavor fail to express feelings of deep alienation from the mainstream of life and its enjoyment. "The competitive life is a lonely one," wrote Philip Slater, "and its satisfactions are very short lived indeed, for each race leads only to a new one."[2]

People come and go. Yesterday they were here, tomorrow they are gone. A study of the lives of successful people is intriguing, and many of them, particularly in the entertainment field, commit what we might call "emotional suicide," and die inwardly long before the body follows suit. The conflicts, inner hurts, and emotional wounds experienced throughout a lifetime accumulate, and eventually the staggering load of this hoard overwhelms its bearer. Usually they seek help first from a psychiatrist, who may delay debilitating effects by assuring the distraught victim that he need not feel insecure for he is not guilty of wrong. He is only a hapless pawn of circumstances. The patient bravely endeavors to believe the analyst and free himself of convicting responsibility, but healing does not result by repeating twenty times a day, "I will not be crushed by this inner weight. I am not guilty. I believe in myself. I am a person of worth, therefore, I can face the world unafraid."

I have watched these people in the world's spotlight who possess natural charisma—athletes, writers, business executives, movie stars, singers, entertainers of various types. The list is endless. Some have come from nowhere, underdogs who ceaselessly strive for success and finally attain it. Others seem to have everything going for them from the beginning and are destined for the top, but never make it. Still others have the mistaken notion that once they are there, nothing can shoot them down. Whatever the philosophy, inner conflict and the individual response to it usually determine the course life takes.

I did not know Freddie Prinze personally, but I watched at close range his struggle with inner conflict. Born in New York of Puerto Rican parentage, Freddie grew up in the ghetto. He was tall, always overweight, considered by everyone a "super nice" person, but not a fighter. A compromiser.

What force drew Freddie Prinze to drugs? His environment? His disposition? Rejection by parents or his peer group? Compensation for being overweight and unpopular? Not really. Freddie was always running from something he was not able to put his finger on. Few people recognized his true emotions—his loneliness, his insecurity arising out of emotionally crippling complexes from being overweight and not able to fight. He joked his way out of difficult situations in an attempt to cover these insecurities. As Freddie grew older, he discovered he had some talent and began to feel that the ghetto was not the place for him, so he lost his sense of belonging.

My only encounter with this lovable young guy was after a crusade. He had read my first book, *Run Baby Run,* and I felt he came with a seeking heart, spiritually sensing that there was something more to life than he seemed able to grasp. He was struggling for that big break all amateurs wait for. Freddie desperately hoped to be discovered as a comedian.

The big break came when he appeared on the Johnny Carson show. Viewers were immediately captivated by Freddie's spellbinding personality and his ability to make them laugh or cry at will. He could reach deep into the hearts of those who were depressed, lift their spirits, and take their minds off their problems.

Johnny Carson was all Freddie needed. In a brief time Freddie rose to popularity, succeeded in losing his excess weight, and made himself presentable to his audiences. He wanted to *be* sharp and *look* sharp—and he succeeded. Fame hit him hard and fast. Tragically, deep within he felt an invisible force, "the kiss of death," following him and poisoning everything he touched. No one could convince him otherwise. Even though his television show, "Chico and the Man," was receiving high ratings, women everywhere were chasing him, he was accepted by all, had everything under control, yet he became more and more confused. He was deteriorating on the inside, broken and searching, and drugs offered an instant, painless escape. So he *thought.*

Although he was only a young man of twenty-two who had hardly begun life, he was now hounded by managers, agents, producers, and lawyers. He didn't have the mind of an executive. How could he at twenty-two? Never sure of which way to turn or what to do, he increasingly sought refuge in drugs, mainly cocaine, in spite of the sound advice of many friends.

One of those friends, Paul Anka, a popular singer in his time, urged Freddie to get away from the confusion and swift-moving world of stardom. Paul's almost disastrous experience reinforced the intensity of his plea with Freddie. He related to Freddie how he suddenly began to lose his identity. Every area of his life became affected, and when it became apparent that he was headed for a breakdown and the loss of his wife and children, he removed himself from the public eye to "get his act together." Withdrawing into isolation, he meditated on life, himself, and true values, and tried to determine what he really wanted. While alone, he discovered that money and fame weren't enough, and that man cannot live by externals alone. When he could handle it, Paul came back stronger than ever and he was able to cope with the forces that almost destroyed him.

But that was Paul Anka. Freddie Prinze did not listen. Slowly he sank into deep depression from which none of his friends, or the best psychiatrist available, could lift him. As the depression deepened, he began jokingly to point his finger like a gun at his head, looking in the mirror, laughing, and telling his friends he probably would die young. His friends laughed, too. Freddie really wasn't joking—he was trying to communicate something from deep within that haunted him continually.

His manager tried to pull him out of this depression by telling him about all the women who literally adored him and would give anything to be near him. "That's the last thing I want to hear," he'd declare. "Don't you understand? I'm dying. I'm dying inside right in front of your very eyes."

Freddie Prinze spoke the truth. Soon he put the gun to his head, pulled the trigger, and ended his life.

Time and space do not permit the mention of all who come to mind, for the list is endless. Elvis Presley, for instance, was a slave of his own fame, and the shadow of loneliness overpowered him. One day when the world least expected it, Elvis died.

Janis Joplin at the height of her brilliant career mixed alcohol with drugs to end her miserable life. Loneliness doggled her every footstep until she could endure no longer.

Joan Crawford was reported to have died of a heart attack, but it has now been confirmed by reliable sources that she ended her life. "Lonely, bitter, reclusive" the newspaper story described her.

Howard Hughes, with all his millions, suffered acute loneliness for years and died utterly alone and mortally afraid.

Barbara Hutton was a multi-millionairess whose death newspapers recently heralded with the headlines, "Hutton spent life fleeing from loneliness."

We may suppose in our ignorance that there is no loneliness for people who have reached the top, but it is just the same for them as for anyone else. "Loneliness is the feeling of not really mattering to anyone," writes Robert E. Lauder. "This feeling can occur at any time in an individual's life; it can affect the young and the elderly, the busy and the leisurely, the reflective and the unreflective."[3]

Let me say again that the unsaved heart is a lonely hunter. If we are without Jesus Christ, feelings of insecurity and a lack of fulfillment lie deep at the core of our being, whether we are at the bottom or at the top of the humanity heap. Covering these feelings with the proud cloak of success, which seems to say "I've got it all together," doesn't extinguish the emptiness.

How we admire and adulate celebrated people, and we cannot imagine that a single cloud mars their flawless horizon of perfect happiness. When tragedy strkes and our unrealistic image bursts, we can't understand what happened. Our problem is that we are totally ignorant of the enormous price tag attached to public life. When we get to the top, there's no one up there with whom we can share our innermost thoughts and feelings, no one we can trust. As long as we are on the way up, climbing, we are moving, but when we get to the top, there is no place to go. The challenge is over, and we sit up there alone.

Successful people without Christ as their Savior aren't the only sufferers of loneliness, however. Many Christian executives, entertainers, athletes, politicians, and famous personalities are lonely too.

Though I never desired or anticipated public life, even to the extent God has placed me there, I have experienced enough to know the problems and heartbreaks of that life. I have learned also that success does not insulate any person from the ravages of loneliness. In my own personal struggle to escape loneliness, I have acquired a few important ground rules that I work at continually. Let me share them with you:

1. Instead of searching for *people* whom you can trust,

focus entirely on God, who alone is trustworthy. When you fully realize that *God is your source* for everything, you stop expecting more from human beings than they can supply.

2. Regardless of pressures or schedules, take time daily (preferably in the morning) to be alone with God. Systematically read His Word. Pray about every problem whether large or small. The Bible says:

> Don't worry about anything; instead, pray about everything; tell God your needs and don't forget to thank him for his answers. If you do this you will experience God's peace, which is far more wonderful than the human mind can understand. His peace will keep your thoughts and your hearts quiet and at rest as you trust Christ Jesus (Phil. 4:6–7 LB).

3. Learn to say *no.* If you have a tendency to be a "workaholic" (meaning that your only pleasure in life is your work), admit it and begin to deal with it. Strip off nonessential activities that rob you of time with God, time with your family, involvement in church, and necessary recreation.

4. Instead of constantly dwelling on your own problems, reach out to someone else in simple friendship, or a witnessing situation, or a discipling relationship. Expect nothing in return. What you receive may be far greater than what you give.

I share these with you because I had to learn the hard way. When I became a Christian I thought all my problems would be solved. But I had to struggle, with God's help, and He has shown me that even though I am a Christian, and can still be lonely, He is the source of all I need.

Part II

**Can You Be a Christian,
and Still Be Lonely?**

6

Can a Christian Really Be Lonely?

Billy Graham makes a startling observation in his famous sermon entitled "Loneliness." Through his many years of wide contact with people all over the world, he states that, in his opinion, loneliness is the greatest problem facing mankind. Think of it! With the multitude of crushing problems in the world, it's hard to imagine that loneliness ranks ahead of all others. He emphasizes further that loneliness affects not just non-Christians, but Christians as well.

Christians lonely? What a startling statement! Theoretically we *never* should be lonely. Jesus Christ, that Friend above all friends who said "I will never leave you nor forsake you" (Heb. 13:5), is living within us. We have resources to draw on that non-Christians know nothing about.

Second, we have a family identity. We have been "born again" into the family of God, which makes us children of God and brothers and sisters of all His redeemed children throughout the world. We share the transforming miracle of sins forgiven and a common heritage so rich that we should cherish each other. What love and devoted fellowship could be ours. God intended it to be that way.

It's no secret, however, that such is not the case. We can't help but notice that the family of God behaves much like biological brothers and sisters do. Criticism, jealousy, squabbling, a competitive spirit abound in Christian circles. *We love each other,* we insist. *We just don't like the way those other Christians act.* So we excuse careless, selfish treatment of our spiritual family and wonder why we are so lonely.

Someone humorously quipped that when people ask, "How's the world treating you?" it's a great temptation to answer, "Oh, the world's treating me fine. It's just those Christians." We laugh, but on the inside we cry because the truth hurts.

My own experiences as a young Christian serve to illustrate what I am saying. Since I had no preconceived notions or previous history to color my expectations, I anticipated near perfection.

Three months after my conversion in St. Nicholas Arena, I decided to attend a Bible College. I don't know what I expected when David Wilkerson told me what Bible College was like because I could think of nothing except the opportunity to learn more of my beloved Savior. It did not occur to me that I would undergo severe culture shock. Although I wasn't traveling to a foreign country, the asphalt jungle from which I came was as foreign a country as the wilds of Africa compared with Bible College. To say that I was totally unprepared might be the understatement of my lifetime.

Perhaps I envisioned some sort of heaven populated with angelic beings. The only two Christians I had known so far, David Wilkerson and a man I met on the airplane while traveling to Bible College, were the personification of what I imagined a Christian ought to be. How did I know there was anything else? Since these two men loved me in Christ just as I was, how could I guess this would not always be the case? Blissfully unaware that the stench of the ghetto and my former life as a savage hoodlum had not worn off, I didn't realize that many professing Christians couldn't look beneath the mere earthen shell to see the light of Jesus burning brightly inside.

From earliest recollections, I had experienced nothing but rejection. No one loved me. No one accepted me. I had bullied my way through life trying to attain acceptance of some sort. Within my gang, I received recognition—yes, even acceptance. Inside of me, however, the aching void of loneliness and misery never subsided. Only in Jesus Christ had I found true acceptance. He knew about my miserable past, my failures, my rottenness through and through—yet He loved me anyway. Now I was going to a place filled with forgiven sinners just like myself. They would love me, too. What happened to me in that new environment might have been easier if I had anticipated imperfection of any sort.

California, I discovered, was a *long way* from New York. Not only that, it was a *far cry* from big city life as well. La Puente, the tiny town at the end of my wearisome journey, was ideally situated in the middle of lovely orchards, peacefully grazing animals, large acreages, and impressive mountains. It was dark at night, and quiet—*very* quiet. A perfect setting, to be sure. But my inner programming during the past few years hadn't included any of those coveted amenities. Instead, I was accustomed to life in the center of New York City—Times Square—the hub of seething, tumultuous activity. Clanging, screeching trains, milling crowds, never-ending traffic noises, brightly lighted streets, all-night haunts, and people, people, people, had been my world. I couldn't make the transition all at once and settle down inside.

In addition, the food and climate in my native country didn't come close to resembling what my body had grown used to. I missed rice and beans and the way meat was cooked with spicy seasonings. I missed the humidity in this dry climate. My skin felt drawn and cracked. My table manners were nonexistent and I probably reminded some people of a voracious animal. No one ever told me that the object of eating was *not* getting the food from the plate to the mouth in the quickest way possible, and it seemed a foolish waste of time when I heard one is not supposed to talk with the mouth full.

Authority? What was that? My first lesson came the day after I arrived. Unfortunately, I appeared a week before school began. Having been in conflict with authority most of my life, I had resolutely determined to stay out of trouble in Bible College. What I didn't know at that early stage of my Christian life was that *rebellion is an attitude, not an act.* My determination focused entirely in the direction of "cleaning up my act," which, of course, left my attitude untouched. So it's no wonder I tangled with the first teacher I met.

"Nicky, since you have time before school opens, I'd like for you to clean the auditorium," this overbearing teacher ordered. At least, that's how I understood it.

"Listen, man," I retorted in my usual manner, "I came here to study—not clean auditoriums. Who do you think I am, the janitor?"

The teacher abruptly turned and walked away. Immediately something within my conscience stabbed at me. The only thing I knew to do was pray. "Lord, I really feel that teacher was out of line to expect me to work for nothing," I began. "Besides, I really did come here to study and learn more about You. You know that."

The longer I justified myself before the Lord, the deeper His knife plunged. Finally I said, "All right, Lord, I guess You want me to do it. I will." He withdrew His knife immediately, and my heart was filled with joy. Thus began my first lesson in submission to authority.

After finding the teacher, I apologized and assured him I would begin the next morning with the clean-up duties. And I experienced a new freedom. The following day I spent fourteen hours mopping floors, cutting grass, trimming trees, and arranging chairs. As I worked, I sang aloud—and I really can't sing. I'm glad the Lord requires only a "joyful noise," for that's all I've ever managed.

That week passed quickly, and the first day of school, which I eagerly anticipated, finally arrived. Scrutinizing the students closely, I began to feel out of place. It became obvious that I was cast from a different mold and was one of a kind, and my kind didn't go to Bible College. I felt even more displaced when the entire student body convened in the auditorium I had worked so hard to clean, and the Dean of Students acquainted us with the school regulations.

My head was swimming—don't do this, don't do that —you must do this, you must never do that. Remember always to protect the reputation of the school. On and on it went until I cried out in my spirit, *What am I doing here? This isn't what I came to learn. Or to protect the reputation of a school. I have enough problems of my own.* It was only my first day, and already I felt like running back to New York to a life I understood. If New York hadn't been so far away, I might have tried it.

My first year could have been a disaster if it hadn't been for Rosalie and Gene. They were the only two in the entire school who risked befriending the "oddball of the campus" who jitterbugged instead of walked, talked too loud, had bad manners, and really didn't belong in a respectable gathering. Instead of the love and understanding I anticipated, I found the rejection—a little more subtle and on a more refined level, but, however you slice it, it was still rejection. And the loneliness returned. Had I ever been this lonely, even in the ghetto?

Rosalie understood. Not because she had been where I had, but because she grew up in New York. Hers was a sheltered life with a minister father, but she attended the same sort of public schools where I became a high school dropout. She knew the drug scene, knew what the gangs were like, and she realized the hurt of peer rejection hidden deep inside of me. She was more compassionate because she knew the language of the ghetto, but in her maturity and solid commitment to Jesus Christ, she saw nothing attractive in it at all. I knew God sent her to school that year just for me.

Even though our relationship was purely friendship, the kind of healthy thing I desperately needed in order to learn for the first time in my life that it is possible to have a platonic association with girls, nevertheless, such a friendship was strictly against the rules. The rules . . . the rules . . . always the rules! Most of the time Rosalie had to write letters of encouragement to me when she knew I was hurting, so we wouldn't get in trouble.

One day I knew I couldn't go on. A series of misunderstandings and consequent punishment hurt me so badly that I couldn't prepare for a forthcoming test. I needed someone to talk to, but there was no one. Little did I know that while I was emptying trash and doing my chores, Rosalie was intently watching from a concealed spot.

"Pssst!" she whispered, daring to break rules to reach out to a suffering fellow student. "Nicky, what's the matter with you?"

"I'm thinking about New York and my friends, Rosalie," I said dejectedly. "I feel so out of place here—no one really loves me—and I have to pretend I'm happy so I won't show what's really on the inside. I'm so lonely I could die."

"I understand, Nicky." Her eyes were full of hurt as she knowingly shook her head, "I understand."

"You know, Rosalie," I continued, "I used to have to cover up my true feelings in the gang, and I find myself doing exactly the same thing here. When I was hurting inside, I just pretended a toughness, a macho image to cover up. Now that I'm a Christian, should I still be doing this? Where are friends who can help me? Everyone here seems so spiritual, I wouldn't dare tell them what's going on inside of me. I've got lots of questions—I really do—and no one to answer them. You can't talk here because no one understands. I pray about it, but I just feel despair inside." I poured out my heart to this girl whose friendship I was denied because of school rules.

"Yes, Nicky. I understand," Rosalie repeated. "I too am always on guard for fear I might say or do the wrong thing. My parents and friends are a long ways away, and sometimes I feel I don't belong here either."

"*You,* Rosalie," I gasped. "I can't believe that."

"Yes, me, too, Nicky. That's why I understand so well." Then she bowed her head and said, "Let's pray, Nicky, and tell the Lord about it." Rosalie cried as she asked the Lord to strengthen and help me. "I want to be your friend and help you, Nicky," she said afterward with tear-filled eyes.

Now I could study for my exam. Someone understood, even if we had to break the rules to share that understanding.

A new revelation was beginning to dawn on me. If just *one* person understands, accepts, and loves you anyway, loneliness diminishes. I now realize that if it had not been for that one person, Rosalie, I might have washed up in my Christian training almost before solidly starting. Knowing that someone cared if I made it or not helped me through many a rough situation.

Something I didn't fully realize in my spiritual youthfulness, however, was the necessary process of growth. I knew I was "born again" into God's family. There was not the slightest hint of doubt in my mind that I was a full-fledged child of God. My changed desires and goals could only be the result of an inner miracle. But I wanted to be perfect. And I expected other Christians to be perfect also. Undoubtedly these unrealistic expectations created further misery in my loneliness at Bible College.

In spite of my earlier resolve to stay out of trouble that first year of Bible College, I wasn't successful. Oh, I'd had little skirmishes now and then, but I saved the big one for the last few weeks before summer break.

For some time I had been watching a humble, sweet-spirited little guy from Mexico—Manuelito. My attention was drawn to him because the kids made fun of him and verbally abused him. Although he was extremely intelligent, he came from the poorest imaginable element in Mexico. His clothing was unbelievably old and outdated, and he did sometimes appear rather ridiculous—but I felt sorry for him and often gave him some of my clothes. He wasn't a fighter, so he avoided retaliation, choosing rather to silently endure the ridicule. I wanted to tell him to not let everyone take advantage of him and that he should stand up to them. I wanted to assure him also that he wasn't second class and inferior, so I began to pray that the Lord would lead me. I could make matters worse by saying the wrong thing if I wasn't careful.

Meanwhile, a big-mouthed, six-foot bully began to push Manuelito around. He was a ball player, arrogant, proud, and critical. He was from a middle-class background and that gave him the idea he was superior. John was a sharp guy, but he knew it and wouldn't let anyone else forget it. He didn't impress me, though.

After taking a shower one afternoon, I headed down the hall to the big dormitory room for a towel to dry my hair when I heard it. John was making fun of Manuelito, and the little fellow just sat on his bunk with his head down.

"Hey, don't do that!" I rushed up to John and spoke with authority. "Don't hurt him that way."

"And just who do you think you are to come in here and order me around?" John demanded as he pushed me away.

"I'm nobody!" I snapped. "But I don't like what you're doing. Lay off!"

As we glared at each other, we must have resembled a big elephant and a small ant. I had handled guys bigger than that, though, and I wasn't afraid of this troublemaker. Besides, he didn't know about my immediate colorful past. I hadn't told anyone.

"You Puerto Rican," he snarled through clenched teeth, "go on back to New York."

That did it! The old Nicky, whom I'd carefully kept in check all these months, broke out and cursed him. He was shocked. His eyes grew wide and he stared speechlessly. I wasn't finished either. I jumped him before he had time to recover, and was ready to smash him in the face when a thought occurred to me—*If I had a baseball bat, I could really clobber him.* So I ran out of the room to find one.

He thought I was running away to avoid a beating. He didn't realize how wrong he was until I returned to finish him off. With the pent-up fury of five Puerto Ricans my size, I attacked him. Before I could swing the bat in his direction, however, four guys grabbed me and held me until John could get out.

Naturally, the school officials learned of the episode almost before it happened, and I was called to the office where I was made to explain my behavior.

"You will go immediately and apologize to John," the Dean told me after I had finished my defense.

"No!" I said firmly as I stood my ground. "I wasn't wrong. He was. I will apologize to the Lord, I will apologize to you. But I will *not* apologize to him."

It's a good thing I loved the Lord with all of my heart. Only He could handle this stubborn, rebellious, dirty Puerto Rican, and transform him from a despicable human being to a useful servant of God.

Of course, I apologized to John. Not without a lot of time in prayer, but God showed this feisty scrapper that there is a more excellent way, and though it might take a lifetime to learn, it would be worth every effort. This was my first painful lesson.

When I finished that first year of Bible College and headed back to New York to work with David Wilkerson, I wasn't certain I ever wanted to return. Not just because I had been lonelier than I could ever remember, but somehow, deep in my spirit, I knew that lonely Christians had to be a contradiction of God's purpose for the body of Christ. I had grasped the scriptural truth of that body intellectually, but it was a deep disappointment to discover that it didn't really exist. And in the very place it should have been on grand display—Bible College.

So what am I saying now? Let's spell it out in clear terms.

Christians never should be lonely, but they are. Millions of them, old and new alike, experience the gnawing emptiness of loneliness day in and day out.

What can the lonely Christian do to alleviate his pain? There are no easy answers to the problem, but we will consider a few constructive steps to take in that direction. The psalmist of old experienced acute loneliness and wrote volumes on the subject. Notice what he said in Psalm 38:6, 8, 11–12 (LB):

> My days are filled with anguish. I am exhausted and crushed; I groan in despair. My loved ones and friends stay away . . . even my own family stands at a distance. Meanwhile my enemies are trying to kill me. They plot my ruin and spend all their waking hours planning treachery.

That's a pretty lonely position, isn't it? How did the psalmist solve his problem? Although he found a number of solutions that he records throughout his writings, we will draw from them a few important principles.

1. Learn to trust God completely. This is a growth—a process that takes time.

> *Commit* thy way unto the LORD; *trust* also in him, and he shall bring it to pass (Ps. 37:5).

To *commit* your loneliness to the Lord is the first step of this growth process. After that comes the day-by-day trust that your answers will come in God's own time. They will not come all at once. That's what makes the process difficult. It's hard to trust God when you're not seeing much happen. But that's what trust is all about.

For we walk by faith, and not by sight (2 Cor. 5:7).

2. Pursue patience. To be impatient is a very human characteristic. When we commit our problems to the Lord, we want answers *now.* We don't want to wait. We are like the familiar story of the man who prayed, "Lord, teach me patience—and teach me right now."

Again as we look to the Psalms we hear David say:

I waited *patiently* for the LORD, and he inclined unto me, and heard my cry (Ps. 40:1).

Rest in the LORD, and wait *patiently* for him (Ps. 37:7).

3. Learn to obey God instead of deferring to your own desires, or doing what seems best in any given situation. Over and over the psalmist emphasizes this important lesson:

I delight to do thy will, O my God; yea, thy law is within my heart (Ps. 40:8).

The law of God is in his heart; none of his steps shall slide (Ps. 37:31).

4. A useful aid to incorporating the above lessons into your daily life is to begin a consecutive reading of the Psalms and turn each verse into a prayer of your own. In other words, pray through the Psalms. In times of deep distress, this has helped me more than anything else.

I'm sure you will find these four suggestions helpful, but we must go a step farther. I discuss this—Him—in our next chapter.

7

The Next Big Step

A Christian should *never* be lonely. We have already established that fact. Also, we touched briefly on the reasoning behind the statement, but so much depends on this truth that we cannot leave it undeveloped.

If Jesus Christ lives within *every* born-again believer in the person of the Holy Spirit, then His divine companionship can fill any aching void that exists when we are denied the comforting presence of friends and loved ones. Why do we not always feel that life operating within us? If, indeed, the Holy Spirit resides in us, why doesn't He make Himself known when we feel so alone and in need of comfort? Is it true that we receive *all* of the Holy Spirit when Jesus Christ becomes our Savior? What problem exists that causes our daily experience to be in such sharp contrast with what the Word of God teaches?

The Bible clearly commands in Ephesians 5:18 that every believer "be filled with the Spirit." Billy Graham writes that "anyone who is not Spirit-filled is a defective Christian. Paul's command to the Ephesian Christians, 'Be filled with the Spirit,' is binding on all of us Christians everywhere in every age. There are no exceptions. We must conclude that since we are ordered to be filled with the Spirit, we are sinning if we are not filled."[1]

Since every believer receives all of the Holy Spirit at the time of salvation (He is a person, and a person cannot be divided), the question seems to hinge on whether or not the Holy Spirit receives all of us. ". . . Our failure to be filled with the Spirit constitutes one of the greatest sins against the Holy Spirit."[2]

What happened to me during my second year of Bible College was the beginning of a new walk of faith, and, also, the beginning of the end of loneliness. I knew I had received Jesus Christ as my Savior, for I had experienced what the Bible said, "When someone becomes a Christian he becomes a brand new person inside. He is not the same anymore. A new life has begun" (2 Cor. 5:17 LB). But I was not walking in the kind of overcoming power I knew I should be, so I began earnestly to seek the reason.

The first step came at an unwelcome hour. Four o'clock in the morning, to be precise. *What's wrong with me?* I agonized within. *Why am I awake? Why am I crying?*

Awakened out of deep sleep and drenched in my own tears, I suddenly heard a voice deep inside of me saying, "Nicky, I'm waking you so you will never forget what I'm telling you right now. I'm calling you, Nicky—setting your life aside for special service to Me. You are going to tell others about the love of Jesus for them."

"But what about *my* plans, Lord?" I quickly protested.

"Your plans are not My plans, Nicky," came the firm answer.

The next three hours were agonizing as I wrestled with the Lord. *Was it really God talking to me, or did I just imagine it?* Just prior to this I had become more sensitive to the Lord and more burdened for my old friends to come to know Him. Maybe that was the reason for this sudden encounter. Perhaps it was all a dream.

Besides, I reasoned further, I was ill-equipped to be any kind of instrument for God. My racial background was a huge strike against me. Being a member of an oppressed minority group, especially Puerto Rican, whose numbers had been greatly abused in this country, was an insurmountable handicap. Why would anyone listen to me? Maybe I could work on my Spanish and go to South America. Didn't *they* need evangelists? It was evident to all that I could hardly express myself in English, so new was the language to me, and I could tell that most people had to work at understanding my heavy accent.

Then I began to ask myself, "Who am *I* anyway? How could I do this? I'm an ex-gang leader, a high school dropout who is having a really tough time in Bible College. I'm probably not smart enough, among other things." I began to feel very depressed thinking God had called me to an impossible task.

All at once God reminded me of Moses. Most of the Bible characters were unknown to me, but I had recently met Moses. *He made excuses, too,* I remembered. *Now, let's see, what were they?* I snapped on my light and opened my Bible. One by one I reviewed them:

"Who am I that I should go?" Moses argued with the Lord. "What will I say to them?"

Hmm, did Moses say that, too? I was startled for a moment.

"They won't believe me," Moses continued, "nor listen to my voice."

How strange! Moses had lived several thousand years ago, but he was saying the same things I was thinking.

"Oh, my Lord, I am not eloquent. . . . I'm slow of speech." So far I had batted 100 percent. Moses and I were two of a kind.

When I came to his last argument, however, I realized I hadn't hit that one yet—*Lord, please send someone else.* I was close to it, though.

Finally, by seven o'clock I was exhausted with the struggle. I knew in my heart that God had spoken, and who was I to resist the living God?

"Yes, Lord. I will do what You want me to do. I am no one, I can't speak English clearly, and I don't know much —but I am Yours. Use me however You desire." Peace flooded my heart. The hand of God was on me, and from that day I was called a man.

What I just described was the commitment of my life to serve the Lord wherever and however He chose. Now I was saved *and* set aside for full-time Christian service. I knew where I was headed. My studies at the Bible College took on greater importance; I exercised more discipline in wholly following the Lord; I became more conscientious than ever in my daily devotional life.

In spite of all I did, however, I knew I was missing much of what God intended for me in my life. Some days I felt close to the Lord and very "spiritual." Other days I was discouraged, defeated, spiritually indifferent, and powerless. On those "other days" depression settled in, chilling my spirit and overwhelming me with the pain of loneliness. I could hardly function as a human being.

I was experiencing what Sherwood Wirt wrote about when he said that "it is possible to be an active, practicing, Bible-loving, Christ-honoring Christian and not be filled with the Spirit and with love, because for years that was precisely my condition.

"I loved Jesus! I loved to think about him and sing about him! But I was frustrated, like a sports car I once observed during an Arizona flood, trying to cross a railroad bridge on the ties."[3]

Although I had heard about the Holy Spirit, I was totally ignorant up until that time of His person, work, and function within the believer. "Jesus loves you" was the haunting message that drew me to God in the first place, so I had concentrated all my efforts in getting to know Jesus better. Now it was time to be introduced to the One who attracted me to the Savior in the first place.

It wasn't a course in school, or a book, or a sermon. The beginning was merely a longing within for more of the Savior. A reaching out and not being able to grasp the fullness of His love. A hungering and thirsting to live an obedient life, but finding little power to do so. Now that I had completely left behind the big, blatant, "gross" sins of the world, I was struggling with subtle, intangible, "Christian" sins and finding defeat a common and discouraging bedfellow. My heart was filled with a sincere desire not to fail my Lord, nor follow afar off, but I was doing it anyway.

So all on my own I began reading the Book of Acts. I remembered someone saying in a chapel service that this book should have been entitled "The Acts of the Holy Spirit." That seemed the logical place to begin. What power those early men of God displayed! Where did it come from? "But you will receive power when the Holy Spirit comes on you; and you will be my witnesses . . ." (Acts 1:8), the book said. There it was! The Holy Spirit.

My search became more clearly defined now. I tracked down all the references I could find that mentioned the Holy Spirit, and I learned a number of things.

I already knew that He lived within me. David Wilkerson had taken great pains to make that point clear. At the time it meant little to me, because I was so ignorant of spiritual truth. However, that fact came back to me. It was confusing at first, because if I had the Holy Spirit inside, why was my life so different from what the Bible said it should be? I couldn't rest until I had the answer.

The Bible called the Holy Spirit the *Comforter.* How I needed comfort in a heart that was so desperately lonely and filled with defeat. Why didn't I have it?

Then I noticed that the Holy Spirit is our *teacher.* The Bible said I didn't need anyone to teach me, for He would do it, and He would bring into my remembrance everything that was stashed away in my brain. Was that really true? I was having a rough time in school, and I certainly could use help of this sort.

Convict of sin. This was no surprise to me. I was under such heavy conviction of sin that it depressed me. Many times during that year of Bible College I was tempted to leave because I felt so unworthy. A Christian lawyer's aide was sacrificing to keep me there, and I knew I was letting him down. I had even written a long letter telling him how tough it was and that I had made a mistake in coming. If I stayed in school, I carefully penned, I was afraid he would be embarrassed; therefore, would he please send me a plane ticket home. Imagine my surprise at his reply:

Dear Nicky:

Glad to hear you are doing so well. Love God and flee Satan. Sorry we have no money in the budget right now. I will write later when we get some money.

Your friend, David.[4]

Trapped! Whenever things got unbearable before, I always ran away. This time I couldn't. I didn't even have money enough to get out of town—if dinky, little La Puente could be called a town. I was sunk if the Holy Spirit couldn't help me. But I had to discover how to get this help, so my search continued.

Although I knew I had been saved by faith, I had been trying to live the Christian life by my own effort. God knew I was struggling and working to be the best Christian I knew how to be. I was conscientious to confess and repent of each sin—selfishness, unforgiveness, a bad temper, irritability, any dishonesty. Then I would determine not to do it again and began working to get rid of the bad habit. I thought this was what Christians were supposed to do. The more I tried to deal with individual sins in my life, though, the worse it became. I felt like a drowning person trying to bail out a boat full of water with a teacup.

In desperation I tore from my notebook several sheets of paper and began to make a list of every sin I could remember. I asked the Holy Spirit to help me, for I didn't want to leave off a single sin. This repentance period was so real to me that it took four days and nights. I discovered much self-will, secret indulgences, deep resentment and resultant bitterness of heart that had never been dealt with, and lack of discipline. I slept and ate little, sat like a zombie in classes, and was unable to prepare any of my studies. Until this matter was settled, I couldn't continue school anyway.

When finally the list was complete, I brought it to the Lord, laid it before Him, told Him I was helpless to handle the sin in my life and be the person He wanted me to be, and surrendered everything I was or ever expected to be. Mentally, I placed myself unconditionally on God's altar and committed myself wholly to Him. I knew immediately that God had accepted my sacrifice, and I was now ready to ask the Holy Spirit to fill me.

"If you then, though you are evil, know how to give good gifts to your children," the Bible says, "how much more will your Father in heaven give the Holy Spirit to those who ask him" (Luke 11:13 NIV).

I had asked before, but nothing had happened. This time was different, however. I had conclusively dealt with sin in my life, and I knew God was ready to cleanse me, transform me, and fill me with the power I lacked. All that was left for me to do was to *believe* He had filled me and give Him permission to go to work and clean up my life.

While a great inner peace replaced the turmoil that had plagued me for so long, I instinctively knew this was just the beginning of a new walk. It was a walk of faith, however, and not the struggle of previous months. Freedom and a new joy flooded my heart, and the Holy Spirit took control of the life that had been so unmanageable.

You can undoubtedly see that the *filling* of the Holy Spirit is a definite experience, but the believer has the daily choice of whether or not to *walk* in the Spirit. Herein lies the path of victory over loneliness. It is possible to be a Christian, even a Spirit-filled Christian, and still be lonely.

Our only hope in this battle against loneliness, or any other battle for that matter, is to be constantly energized by the Holy Spirit. If we would experience continual victory in our lives, we must *live* and *walk* in the Spirit. We run back and forth between flesh and spirit and wonder why we are constantly defeated. The truth is that we are afraid to allow God full control.

For some unimaginable reason, we have this twisted, warped idea that if we surrender fully to God, He will take away everything we want to do and force us to do the things we don't want to do. What a preposterous notion! God tells us in His Word that if we delight ourselves in Him, "He will give you all your heart's desires" (Ps. 37:4 LB). And that includes victory over loneliness, praise His name!

Let me summarize what I've tried to say in this chapter: It is possible for the Christian to overcome loneliness in his life, but he does not have the power in himself. Only as he experiences the filling of the Holy Spirit and daily walks in the Spirit can he hope to defeat this enemy giant.

How can we be filled with the Holy Spirit? As I analyzed the Scriptures and my own experience, I found that five important steps were necessary.

1. *Deal conclusively with sin in your life.* Not just one or two sins, but everything that could be considered in the light of Hebrews 12:1 which says, "Let us lay aside every weight, and the sin which doth so easily beset us."

Bertha Smith, dear old veteran missionary to China who is well into her eighties, insists upon a sin list. "Write them out," she demands in her fiery, high-pitched voice. "If it takes a week or a month, don't stop until God tells you you're finished. You can never be filled with the Holy Spirit until you reckon with everything in your life that displeases God."

When the sin list is finished, *confess* them one by one in the light of 1 John 1:9. "If we confess our sins, he is faithful and just to forgive us our sins, and to cleanse us from all unrighteousness." *Make restitution* where it is needed. Do not rest until every shadow of darkness in your life is washed away in the blood of Jesus.

2. *Surrender everything you are and have to God.* "Not all who preach consecration are consecrated people," Watchman Nee says. "Not all who understand the doctrine of consecration know the reality of consecration."[5] Lay everything down unconditionally. Take everything to the altar. Romans 12:1 tells us to "present your bodies a living sacrifice, holy, acceptable unto God." "The meaning of the altar is the offering up of the life to God to be ever consumed. God wants these lives of ours consecrated to Him that throughout their entire course they may be ceaselessly being consumed for Him."[6]

3. *Ask the Holy Spirit to fill you.* ". . . How much more shall your heavenly Father give the Holy Spirit to them that ask him?" (Luke 11:13).

The disciples were instructed to "tarry . . . in the city of Jerusalem, until ye be endued with power from on high" (Luke 24:49). They didn't dare go forth without that power. And neither do we dare to face life with all its complexities and hurts and fears without that power.

4. *Believe that God has done exactly what He said He would do.* Perhaps the greatest misunderstanding lies right here. We believe only when we *feel* filled with the Spirit. Feelings have nothing to do with God's performance of His promise. What He has *said,* that will He do—so "if God said it, that settles it!" Refuse to consult your feelings, for they are always inaccurate indicators of the truth. Simply believe God's promise, because He cannot lie.

5. *Give God permission to go to work in your life.* The occasion of being filled with the Holy Spirit is simply the *first step* of a whole new life of faith. Many people fall into great

disillusionment because they think they have arrived at perfection. No longer will they have to struggle with sin or temptation. Such is *not* the case. That initial step of faith does not instantly transform your tastes and desires. It is a step-by-step process as you yield each moment to the Spirit's control.

I have found out that being saved and being filled with the Holy Spirit are similar in one respect—neither one necessarily guarantees you the absence of trouble in your life. Even though I had new power I still realized a day-to-day struggle in my life.

8

Which Way Shall I Turn?

The ultimate solution to loneliness, without question, is being filled with the Holy Spirit and always walking in the power of the Spirit. Knowing this is one thing. Doing it is not always so easy.

As I travel throughout the world and counsel Christians everywhere, one of the questions I am asked repeatedly is, "How can I be certain I am in God's will? How do I find God's will for my life?"

So much confusion surrounds the mystery of God's will that I have concluded being out of God's will, or thinking you might be, is a lonely problem. Questions are generated for which there seem to be no answers. Consider these, for instance:

Can a Christian take on too much responsibility and become so disheartened and discouraged in the work of the Lord that he presumes he missed God's will in the first place?

Is it possible for a sincere Christian to be in the wrong place even though he honestly believes he was divinely led and it was God's will for him?

Or, are these two situations a contradiction in terms?

Yes, they are! The trouble is that theory and reality don't always match, and conscientious Christians often find themselves in the puzzling dilemmas suggested above. Sadly enough, this is the plight of the more earnest believer rather than the one whose chief desire is to escape hell and somehow make it to heaven.

How does a Christian find God's will? I am speaking of the kind of Christian we discussed in the last chapter—the Spirit-filled one, the totally committed one, the sold-out one.

Probably one of the darkest periods in my young Christian life centered around the questions above. Shortly after graduation from Bible College, I married the most beautiful girl and the sweetest Christian I had ever met. Gloria and I became acquainted at college, together sought God's will for our relationship, and together felt called of God to a specific ministry. We were so poor at that time that even the poor people pitied us. But we didn't know it. We both felt exceedingly rich because we had each other and a rich Father. What more could anyone ask?

Our honeymoon was cut short by limited funds and the beginning of a crusade in which I was to preach. Two days were all we could spare, but we were starting life together with exactly the right preparation for our entire marriage. It would always be that way. God's calling first, personal interests last. Not that we always wanted it so. It just turned out that we had little choice.

David Wilkerson was now deeply involved in the brawling Teen Challenge Center for teenagers and drug addicts in New York, and he had invited us to be a part of his ministry. My beginning salary of $10 a week plus room and board didn't dampen my enthusiasm. Wasn't it more than I'd had for three years? And wasn't it a priceless privilege to handle the unsearchable riches of Christ and be paid for doing the thing I desired more than life itself?

Three years passed in that exciting, demanding, life-changing outreach ministry. I never tired of sharing my Savior with those pathetic, misdirected people whose lives at such a young age were destroyed by drugs and crime. Since almost all of them were victims of broken homes, parental rejection, and total absence of human love in their lives, I could identify deeply. Often I wept bitterly as I heard their stories. Many were kicked out of homes by alcoholic mothers who were more interested in the succession of men they entertained each night, or were beaten daily by uncaring stepfathers. Most were abused physically, sexually, or emotionally by older family members. Where else but to the streets, drugs, and prostitution could they turn? My heart ached for them.

For three years I gave myself tirelessly to these misfits. The Wilkersons had moved during the first year to Staten Island, and David commuted each day to supervise the work at the center. Gloria and I took the apartment on the second floor of the three-story building where we housed forty narcotic addicts in separate men's and women's dormitories. The work grew by leaps and bounds, but so did the problems.

Our first baby, Alicia Ann, was born after we moved into the larger apartment. Gloria had been working with the women, but now she was fully occupied with our new little daughter. More and more, with the ministry expanding into other locations, David's presence at the center diminished. The full weight of responsibility fell on me. There was no time for my family, recreation of any kind, or even days off to refresh myself physically and mentally. I became exhausted, depressed, and too discouraged to continue. I tried to tell David what I was feeling, but his own ministry involvements were so heavy he either didn't hear or couldn't manage another problem himself. "You can handle it, Nicky," he always said with a reassuring smile. "I have utmost confidence in you."

Usually I went away from these sessions encouraged,

lifted up for a while. My deepest desire was to believe in and please this man of God to whom I owed everything. But the problems at the center only worsened, it seemed, and the unspeakable nature of these problems shattered my deep conviction that "if anyone is in Christ, he is a new creation; the old has gone, the new has come" (2 Cor. 5:17). I couldn't reconcile Scripture with what was happening.

It was discouraging enough to see those who had come to the center professing a salvation experience and then return to old habits of drug addiction, for instance. I understood the stranglehold of heroin on its victims, because I had locked myself in a room several times with fellows kicking the habit. I learned that they were extremely vulnerable for a dangerous period in the weeks following.

Drugs were one thing, but adultery and lesbian and homosexual relationships were quite another, to my way of thinking. Discovering these blatant sins between inmates deeply troubled me, but when they broke out among the staff, I was shaken to the core. One of our staff became involved with a young resident.

My handling of these eruptions no doubt lacked insight due to immaturity, inexperience, and a lack of sympathy. But I had lived only twenty-four years, and I couldn't react with the seasoned mind of a forty-year-old without the advantage of the intervening years to equip me.

Turmoil raged within. There was no one, absolutely no one, with whom I could share my heavy burden. My staff was torn in loyalties. Most of them had come from the streets (who else could work with street people?), so when these blatant sins were exposed by one means or another, some of the staff stood solidly behind me, and some were drawn in sympathy to the offenders. Therefore, my decisions and discipline were questioned. Havoc reigned.

I had trusted my staff implicitly, yet confidential information consistently leaked out, hurting the ministry and persons involved. Everywhere I turned, there were insurmountable problems. I couldn't sleep at night, and although I knew it was not a manly thing to do, I wept profusely. I really wanted to fire the offending staff members, but I couldn't bring myself to do it. Most of them had been converted through the ministry of the center, and though I knew they should not have been given such heavy responsibilities, David often hired people more for compassion than for their ability to work. I became so burdened with other people's problems that I constantly cried to the Lord, "What am I doing wrong? Show me. Please help me."

Gloria could not share the oppressive weight of my load, either. Busy night and day with a demanding infant, she could not be expected to absorb added responsibility, and I could not lay it on her. Naturally, she didn't understand my depression and the ensuing lack of communication between us.

Even the heavens seemed shut. For the first time since I had transferred ownership of my life to Jesus Christ, I could not feel His sweet, comforting presence. Prayer was a mere exercise rather than the precious communication and energizing release it had been. *What did God want me to do in these situations?* I couldn't tell. Either *I* wasn't getting through, or God wasn't. I finally found myself utterly alone. If I thought it had been tough on the streets, or in Bible College, I was unthinkably naive. They were nothing compared with the hopeless dilemma staring at me from every angle.

The only bright spot during those days was my work in Spanish Harlem. Large crowds gathered every time we set up for a street meeting, the Holy Spirit moved in great waves of conviction as considerable numbers came forward to receive Jesus Christ, and the work grew unbelievably. I couldn't go often, though, due to the pressures at the center. Every time I broke away, a major catastrophe awaited my return.

Since it appeared that God's blessing was on nothing

else but this Spanish-speaking ministry, I wanted to open a center predominantly to reach this culture. It was my only hope of survival. It hadn't occurred to me yet to leave the Teen Challenge ministry and look for other opportunities.

Full of hope after a long session of prayer asking God to place His stamp of approval on my plans, I approached David Wilkerson with my idea. He listened thoughtfully, then sat for a long time in deep concentration. His expression was not the eager, receptive agreement I had anticipated. Finally he looked up at me and said slowly, "Nicky, I'll have to pray about this. I don't feel a confirmation in my heart that this is what God wants right now."

Broken in spirit, I left our conference utterly demoralized. I couldn't go on, and I knew it. There was nothing left to give. A heaviness I had never experienced weighted me beyond further endurance.

"Oh, God!" I cried. "I've given all I have to this work. I've even sacrificed my own marriage and precious family. For three years I've placed these sorry people above everything else in my life, and look at them. Look at me! What good did it do?"

My next move seemed inevitable. I resigned my work with Teen Challenge, packed up my few belongings, loaded my family into the car, and headed out.

Since California was the only place in the United States besides New York that I was familiar with, this seemed the logical destination. Besides, Gloria's family lived there, and it was like going home in one sense. To us, California seemed a land of opportunity with jobs everywhere.

We had invited fourteen newly converted drug addicts to feed and house for two months until the opening of Bible College, so Gloria and I rolled up our sleeves and pitched in. We had a little money that was given us before leaving New York, and my savings account totaled $1,200. We could weather a brief period without work provided no unexpected gale blew in on our calm sea.

For some reason, though, *everything* went wrong. The fourteen fellows ate like thirty hogs. Gloria became exhausted trying to cook and feed that bunch and lost ten pounds in the process. We spent all our money, and my savings dwindled to $28. *How am I going to pay my rent?* I began to ask myself.

Although the fellows were becoming a financial burden, I couldn't tell them to get out. Hadn't I encouraged them to go to Bible College and invited them to stay with us until the fall semester opened? Inwardly frustrated, I was irritable and touchy. Eventually, because I couldn't *see* that God was making a single move in any direction to help my situation, I became angry with Him, angry with the fellows, angry with Gloria. Most of all, I was furious at myself.

At this point, a period of morbid introspection was launched, and I became engulfed in an ocean of "Why's" and "If only I had . . ." and "Was I wrong?" Guilt washed over me in unrelenting waves as I scoured my conscience for some sin I needed to confess. I knew I had let God down. I searched my soul wanting to correct whatever separated us, but I only grew colder spiritually and more miserable to get along with.

Preaching was the last thing I wanted to do at this juncture. How could I preach without the slightest consciousness of God's presence? There were no opportunities anyway, so undoubtedly God did not intend that for me. *What about my call to evangelism?* In my spiritually dulled state, I could reason that away, too. *I just imagined God called me,* I concluded. *It's obvious now that I was wrong.*

As hunger and desperation drove me, I intensified my search for a job. At first I was a little selective, choosing "respectable" occupations. As every door slammed shut in my face and survival became the issue, I would have taken anything. I'd have dug ditches, picked fruit, washed dishes, cleaned toilets. Nothing was beneath me now. Still I couldn't find a job.

Finally Gloria went looking for work. By then I felt I had failed the Lord, my wife, and my baby so miserably that in my eyes I was a worm crawling. But we had to have money. And we had to have it immediately. Bible College had begun, and we were no longer strapped with the fellows, but we hit rock bottom anyway. Even Gloria couldn't find a job.

Just at the most crucial moment, when it was a choice between starving or begging to provide food for my family, I had an invitation to preach. It really didn't matter that I didn't want to preach. Hadn't I said I would do anything to earn money? Anything included preaching. Out of sheer desperation, I accepted the invitation knowing fully that my spirit was empty.

Having been out of touch with Christian trends for many weeks now, I had no inkling that the newly published book telling the story of my conversion, *The Cross and the Switchblade,* was fast becoming a popular best seller. Its demand was exceeding anything on the Christian book market. So when I appeared, the place was packed out. I was astonished. As I sat on the platform, my heart was smitten with the conviction that my motive for preaching was money, not the love of God or love of souls. Even so, I stood up to preach without an anointing from above.

During the message—right in the middle of it—God convicted me of my sin so strongly that I wasn't sure I could continue. I knew I wasn't worthy of His blessings, worthy of His forgiveness, worthy of His provision. How I finished, I'll never know. Why God blessed, I'll never know. Many came weeping to the Savior after the sermon. All I could do was get away as soon as possible.

With the cash offering in my pocket, my excited heart was like a child clutching a nickel on the way to the candy store. I wanted to take Gloria to a nice, middle-class restaurant, sit there and ask the waitress to bring Gloria whatever she wanted to eat, then watch her as she enjoyed the meal and have her say, "Thank you, Nicky, for taking me out. It was so good." More than anything else, I knew this would boost my sagging ego.

Driving along, having told Gloria my plans, a deep unrest began troubling me. I felt like returning to the apartment to pray. Embarrassed, I explained apologetically to Gloria. "I feel the need to pray, Gloria. I know you're hungry. I am, too. But I don't think I can eat right now. Let's go back to our apartment and just thank God for what He did tonight."

If ever a man knew he had the right wife, I knew it that night.

"Of course, Nicky, that's exactly what we should do," Gloria assured me. "I know you want to take me out to eat, but it's 11:00, you know, and probably nothing is open anyway. Let's go home and have supper with the Lord, Nicky."

For four hours I cried and prayed and poured out the confessions of an unbelieving heart. As I held Gloria's hand, I asked the Lord to forgive me, and told Him over and over that I loved Him more than anything else in all the world. When at last my heart was at peace and I could rise from my knees, Gloria solemnly declared, "Nicky, God has called us both. We had to go through this terrible battle just to know that we can trust God fully. You have been called to preach, and I am standing with you. Together we will do God's will from this moment on."

She was right. From that moment, invitations for crusades began pouring in, and it was as if God's hand of blessing was on me and nothing could reverse it. Except, of course, sin in the life of God's servant. Having emerged from such darkness, however, I was determined that nothing would enter my life again to wreck God's purpose. I knew full well the truth of the Scripture: "Promotion cometh neither from the east, nor from the west, nor from the south. But God is the judge: he putteth down one, and setteth up another" (Ps. 75:6–7). Out of ashes came beauty. From the pits of loneliness and despair, a ministry was born. But God never let me forget the pits.

Looking back on that miserable sequence of events, I realize I was too young in the Lord to analyze what was happening and how to discern God's will for my life. It took many years, much experience, humiliating failures, and a searching heart to learn what was wrong. I desperately wanted to be in the center of God's perfect will, and I knew God wanted me there. Why was I having such trouble finding it?

Now I know. I wanted God's will, but I wouldn't turn loose of my own. Whenever I was faced with major decisions, *I always* prayed. But I *always* knew how it had to be in order to work out right.

One day while wrestling with an important future consideration, the Lord opened my eyes. "Nicky," He said, "you can't know My will until you lay down yours. I won't show you until you are willing to do it whatever it costs you."

Turmoil raged. "But, Lord, I can't see that things would work out any other way except this way," my heart cried.

"What difference does it make whether you see it or not? I am God."

So that was it. Having realized that my will was in the way of finding God's will did not eliminate a fierce battle. Laying down my will was a life-and-death conflict with an enemy cunningly plotting to keep me defeated for the rest of my life. After several skirmishes at different times with the old hound, it became easier. At length, I could quickly say, "Not my will, but Yours."

I finally saw the principle. Before we can ask God to reveal His will, we must get rid of our own. Then, and only then, can we pray for guidance. At that point it's only a short distance to hearing His clear assurance—"this is the way, walk in it."

When a Christian is absolutely certain He is in the center of God's will, many other problems disappear. Loneliness can be one of them. Consider the great patriarchs and other Bible characters. Or think about missionaries in foreign, unfriendly places with no one near to sympathize. The overwhelming conviction that they are exactly where God wants them gives courage to continue and a oneness with their Maker that precludes human companionship.

What do I advise earnest Christians who ask me, "How can I find God's will for my life?" As I have wrestled with the same question myself, the Lord has given me some helpful criteria in determining God's will in every decision whether large or small. Let me list them for you with a simple warning. While they are helpful, they are not infallible except for the first one. Do not isolate any of these suggestions to the exclusion of the others and base your decision accordingly. Here they are:

1. *The Bible.* God's will and God's *Word* never disagree. Search the *Word* of God for clearer understanding.

2. *Circumstances.* Are things falling into place? Are obstacles being removed?

3. *Advice.* Often the prayerful advice of godly people such as your pastor, parents, trusted friend, other family members, etc., gives clearer insight. Listen to them.

4. *Inward impressions.* God's will promotes peace within. Is there anxiety, doubt, fear, confusion? Wait awhile.

5. *Open/closed doors.* Watch for these.

6. *Timing.* Allow God to choose His own. Don't push Him. He is never too late or early. He may want to teach you a little patience, you know.

Often when I am tempted to feel sorry for myself because my little plot in God's vineyard is tough, I remember a passage in one of my favorite books, *The Hiding Place*. Corrie Ten Boom had just gotten out of bed in the middle of a restless night during the war to find her sister, Betsy, downstairs in the kitchen fixing tea. After sharing a brief conversation and a cup of tea, they went back upstairs to try to sleep. Corrie discovered a large piece of shrapnel plunged through her pillow on the very spot her head had rested only minutes before. Terrified, she ran for Betsy. Her sister's classic remark remains in my heart. "Corrie, the only place of safety is in the center of God's will."

Part III

Where Loneliness
Should Never Happen

9

For Better Or Worse, But Not for Good!

"Marriage is characterized in America by much unhappiness."[1] Even Christian marriages! Even Christian marriages where both husband and wife are active in church and are striving to grow spiritually. Even, would you believe, the marriages of Christian leaders—pastors, evangelists, church workers.

"All things considered, marriage today is not a good proposition. In our major U.S. cities during these last several years, applications for marriage licenses and proceedings toward divorce number about the same. *Of all couples marrying in America today, forty percent will be divorced within the next twenty years.*"[2]

Although the growing malignancy of divorce in our society began, for the most part, outside the church among non-Christians, its infection has spread throughout the church and professing Christendom. Not too many years ago I hardly knew of a divorced Christian. Today our churches are so full of divorced singles that not to have a ministry directed to them is to seriously limit the church's effective outreach.

It is no secret that one of the most common problems both of married people and of formerly married is loneliness. I hear it on all sides: "Loneliness is eating my heart out." Loneliness within marriage is used often as reason for divorce, and loneliness of singles is used often as reason for marriage or remarriage. In neither case is this sufficient cause for decision, but loneliness strips us of logic and drives us to unwise action.

My own marriage is going into its nineteenth year, and though Gloria and I have weathered a number of storms, I can honestly say that our marriage is stronger and sweeter today than it has ever been. This is not because we finally are adjusting to each other, or that we are "getting the hang" of living together, or that our four children are binding us to one another. No. "Happy marriages are made, not found,"[3] and we are working hard toward making our marriage what God intends it to be.

Through my years of ministry and the nineteen years of our marriage, I have learned much about keeping a marriage together. Gloria and I have made foolish mistakes and have sought God's wisdom to profit from them; I have observed numbers of married people and have tried to evaluate their problems in the light of God's Word and practical solutions; and I have been called on to counsel countless couples that has forced me to rely on the Holy Spirit for the wisdom God promises when my own is deficient or lacking.

I am not an authority by any stretch of the imagination, but I believe God has given me some insights that I wish to share. They didn't come easily nor without embarrassing mistakes. My first counseling experience, for instance, still causes me to blush.

The beautiful young woman sitting directly across from my desk was in tears. She had come for counseling and was in the process of telling me how miserable her marriage was and why she couldn't possibly remain in it.

"I am so unhappy," she wailed. "Charlie and I have

absolutely nothing in common except our children. We can't communicate, he doesn't like to do the things I like, we can't agree on anything, and we are merely enduring each other."

Since this was my first marriage counseling situation, I knew I was too inexperienced to handle it well. I was scared, too. Not quite thirty years old, I had no business telling someone else how to run her marriage. I was just getting the hang of it myself, so I proceeded cautiously, feeling my way through, and listening more than talking at first.

"When I got married," she continued, "I thought I would have someone to share my life with. You know, someone to laugh with, cry with, bare my deepest feelings, and hopes, and desires. We can't even talk except about the most casual of concerns—the children. Money. When will dinner be ready? That's no way to live. I'm so lonely, I can't go on. I would rather endure anything but this loneliness day after day."

"Tell me," I finally found the courage to speak, "why did you marry this man in the first place?"

"Well, I, uh—I was, uh—I was very young," she stammered. "I thought I loved him."

"Did you love him?" I leveled my eyes with hers.

"I thought so." She became defensive. "Now I realize I didn't understand what love is, and without love there really isn't a true marriage, is there?" She was pressing me to agree.

Ignoring the ploy, I probed further. "Are you a Christian, Virginia? Have you personally invited Jesus Christ into your life to be your Savior?"

"Oh, yes!" she exclaimed. "Without Christ and my church, I couldn't possibly have lasted this long."

"How about Charlie?"

"He *says* he's a Christian, too, but how would I know for sure?" she shrugged her shoulders. "We never discuss anything that deep."

"How does he feel about ending the marriage?" I asked point blank.

"Charlie doesn't even think there's anything wrong in our marriage," she exploded. "Can you believe anyone could be that insensitive?"

"Since you are a Christian, Virginia, you undoubtedly care about God's will for your life and obedience to the Word of God," I said.

"Certainly, or I wouldn't be here talking with you," she snapped. I had hit a sensitive nerve. "Surely you don't think God intended marriage to be like this? And I refuse to believe that God expects me to live this way the rest of my life. You don't know what it's like, Nicky." Her eyes began filling with tears again. "You have no idea what it is to go through day after day, month after month, year after year thinking things will get better, but they never do. I have needs that aren't being met. Charlie's so wrapped up in the success of his business that he doesn't even notice he's not satisfying me as a woman, let alone just simple communication."

I began to be uncomfortable as she described in detail the nature of their physical incompatibility. Does this woman have something in mind other than sound advice from a Christian man? No, certainly not. I'm just imagining such a thing. I put the thought out of my mind and asked the Holy Spirit to give me wisdom.

My office became very warm, and I grew more uncomfortable as she continued. I knew I was not just imagining. Whether she came with ulterior motive or not, I couldn't be sure. I had asked the Holy Spirit for wisdom, and instinctively I knew that this woman was not seeking mere counsel.

Now I was really frightened. What should I do? Stay and try to pull this thing out of the fire and hope to give the woman sound direction? I shot up a quick prayer, and immediately I knew I had to get out. Seizing on a pause in the flow of her dialogue, I cleared my throat, stood up and said, "Excuse me for a few moments, Virginia. I'll be right back."

I walked over to my secretary and whispered, "I need your help, Sandy. Wait about five minutes and then go into my office and explain to the lady sitting there that I have been unavoidably detained. Tell her I'll try to get back to her later in the week."

I grabbed my coat and dashed out into the fresh air to regain mental and physical composure. Having "blown" my first marriage counseling session, I needed to sort out my mixed emotions and thoughts. It wasn't easy for a sincere, eager-to-please-God youthful evangelist to chalk this one up to experience and forget it. Guilt clouded my perspective for a long time.

When the dust settled, and I could see the situation objectively, I drew some sound conclusions as guidelines for future similar predicaments. I understood clearly from this experience that just such circumstances had been the ruin of many a man of God. Moral collapse does not happen overnight. The counseling room often is the spawning ground for these tragedies.

Since God had blessed my ministry far beyond anyone's expectations, most of all mine, I knew His blessing could be removed and placed on another in short order. I knew, also, that Satan was after my ministry—and me. He had already won several rounds in the past, and I had resolved that the path of implicit obedience was going to be my chosen course for the rest of life, no matter how misunderstood I might be.

Therefore, future counseling of women in troubled marriages was not for me. Did I not have godly women on my staff who could handle such problems? In fact, all counseling of women would be delegated to other women experienced in such matters except when Gloria could be with me.

My contribution to ailing marriages would be confined to dealing with couples, husband and wife together. I found this to be far more effective in the long run. Neither could exaggerate or conjure up circumstances that did not exist, and when honesty prevails, much time is conserved.

After many years of earnest marriage counseling, I have come to realize that the loneliest of people in the world are often married people. Confined within the protective walls of a house, such forlorn people weep out the agonizing desolation of their isolated existence.

This loneliness is not confined to non-Christians, either. Since the stigma of divorce is being lifted, Christian marriages are falling apart in epidemic proportions today. Even ministers, evangelists, and Christian leaders of every description are abandoning their marriages for one reason or another, and almost all of them express deep feelings of aloneness, detachment from spouse, or the finding of someone else more compatible, more understanding.

My friend, Bob, found himself in just such a predicament. He was called to Christian ministry during his youth, but like so many other teenagers he wandered away from God and his childhood training. He married a girl whom he knew was not God's will for him, submitting to pressure from an insistent father who thought she was right for him.

Years of unhappiness followed. He resented his young wife because he felt cheated of true happiness and God's will. The divine calling never left him, and he struggled continually with the realization that he had missed God's best for his life.

Finally, when an opportunity for a part-time music ministry in his church opened, Bob took it, and God's blessing rested on his efforts. Realizing that his only joy in life was the time involved with this ministry, he devoted more and more of himself to it. But his young wife, who had not been called to ministry of any sort, grew more dissatisfied and made his life miserable at home. The worse it became, the more Bob sought to escape—to his successful business by day, and his growing music ministry weekends and nights.

Soon his story was typical of millions of Americans

today. They slept in the same house, but they lived their separate lives, hardly ever converging. When they were together, it was only to vent bitterness and air deep-seated, long-standing grievances. Bob hardly knew his two sons. His wife constantly opposed Bob's only source of satisfaction in life—his ministry.

In his heart, Bob desperately desired what he knew was God's original intention for him—full-time Christian ministry. He had opportunities, but he realized it would never work unless his family supported him. It was almost a relief when he returned home from a business trip one day to find a court order evicting him from his home and forcing a separation.

For two-and-a-half years, Bob pursued his ministry alone. At times the loneliness and guilt he experienced were overwhelming. Although he sought a reconciliation with his wife, it was always on her terms—the ministry must go! What was Bob to do? How could anyone advise him? All I could say was, "But for the grace of God, there go I."

Are divorce and remarriage solving our relationship problems? Are they alleviating our feelings of loneliness, meaninglessness, and boredom? The complicated intricacies of every individual marriage problem preclude "pat" answers, and I soon began to realize that I had to prayerfully examine these problems in the light of Scripture if I was going to be used of God in the lives of those who sought my help.

It is true, as so many have reminded me, that times have changed since the inspired writing of the Bible. That inspired account still says, however, "I the LORD do not change" (Mal. 3:6 NIV).

This means that His Word is still the authority by which we measure our decisions if we would walk in obedience.

I knew all the commonly accepted psychological reasons for incompatibility in marriage leading to divorce, such as: the breaking down of close family and community ties;

high mobility; work/residence separation; disintegration of community life; breakdown of the family unit; interchangeableness of home, friends, and communities; pressures of society; isolation felt by the wives of highly mobile professional men—and on and on. These are not solutions, however, and because we are victims, so to speak, of such conditions, we must penetrate deeper to find workable answers. At least Christians should.

. I began to notice in my counseling sessions a similarity of causes for marital discord. Lack of communication was high on the list. Close behind were, "We have absolutely nothing in common—we each go our separate ways and live our separate lives," or "We just don't love each other anymore," or "We weren't right for each other in the first place." Various shadings of these basic reasons were offered in individual cases, but it all boiled down to pretty much the same thing. As I questioned each participant, I sought discernment of the Spirit and inner ears to hear beyond mere words. The real motives, I discovered, were vastly different from what the couples were saying, and I am convinced that in most cases they really were ignorant of these motives. If we say something long enough, whether right or wrong, in time we believe it to be the truth.

Lack of a spirit of obedience is the malignancy that is eating away at the heart of the body of Christ today. The God who made us knows how we operate best, and He said concerning marriage: "What God has joined together, let man not separate" (Matt. 19:6 NIV). Our excuses for walking away from our marriages are, for the most part, refusal to look at the clear Word of God and walk in obedience.

If we have a heart to obey, we will be more careful to wait for God's choice of a marriage partner rather than rushing into a union for fear we might be left out altogether. If we have a heart to obey, we will not enter marriage with the idea that we will stick as long as we can, but when it gets unbearable, we'll run.

Not too long ago, a middle-aged Christian woman came to me for counseling. I called Gloria to sit in on the session with me. She was young looking, trim of figure, obviously fashion conscious, and held a responsible position in a prominent firm.

"You don't know how I've prayed and sought the will of God for my life," she began. "I really feel God is leading me to leave my husband. I simply can't go on in this miserable marriage."

"What seems to be the trouble?" I asked.

"I'm not sure," she said slowly and thoughtfully. "Maybe we were never right for each other, or, maybe I've outgrown him. You see, I have a very fine career. I am a professional in my field. I have grown and expanded through the years, while my husband seems to have remained dormant. We simply are not on the same level anymore, if we ever were. And . . . and I'm just not happy, that's all."

"What kind of happiness are you expecting from your marriage?" I countered. "What is happiness to you?"

"Well, I'm not sure," she replied. "I think I could be happy with a man who was mentally stimulating. Of course, I realize I'm not young anymore, and it may be that no one would be interested in me. But is it wrong to want to be happy for whatever years I have left?"

"Have you considered what the Bible has to say?" I finally asked her after a lengthy discussion on the difficulty of achieving a utopian-type happiness between two very flawed people.

"Yes, I have," she admitted. "But certainly you realize that the Bible was written thousands of years ago. Life was much simpler then, and people didn't face the problems we now have. We cannot apply to present-day situations principles laid down generations ago, can we?"

"Do you think," I countered, "that the God who created men and women and the Holy Spirit who inspired the writing of God's Word did not know, whether in that generation or this, how they function best?"

"Are you trying to put me on a guilt trip?" she answered coldly. "Well, I won't buy it."

The woman refused to answer my question, promptly switched the subject, and soon ended the session. What was her problem? The real problem? It was not the difficulty in her marriage, but the difficulty in her own heart. It was the obvious absence of a spirit of obedience, and no amount of counseling could change the fact that her heart was in rebellion.

Who said marriage is a beautiful Hollywood dream of love and bliss? Not God. Not experience. Marriage, like any other relationship in life, is tough. Every marriage that ever existed sparked problems big enough for its partners to consider divorce. Or suicide. Or murder. Every marriage that ever survived involved overcoming problems. For the Christian the beginning of that overcoming is a heart yielded to the will of God, and a will set to obey.

Of course, there are lonely people who are married. Their number is legion. I shall never forget, however, the heartbreaking statement of a Christian woman who chose divorce and rearing her children alone. She summed up for countless others the bitter reality of her choice when she said, "Nicky, I *thought* I was lonely in a marriage where there was no communication, but I never knew what loneliness was until I left that marriage."

"If you have any choice at all, *don't divorce*. Despite what people may tell you, the life of the formerly married isn't all that glamorous. From the midst of a chaotic marriage, the single life looks peaceful and glamorous: no more nagging, no more frustration, and a whole new world of freedom."[4] Once they are single again, many people find that this is not the case.

Over and over again, I hear, "Sometimes I think I'm going to die from loneliness."

"Weekends are the worst, and often when I am alone on the weekends I start crying and can't stop. I can't even figure out what starts it going," another distraught divorcee told me.

"The loneliest times are in the evenings after I come home from a hard day, so tired and there's no one there. The apartment is quiet and stuffy from being closed up all day. There's no one to say, 'Hey, let's talk, or let's play a game of Scrabble, or watch the tube.' It's *so* quiet," a young divorced bachelor said.

Loneliness can kill you, a prominent psychologist, James J. Lynch, concluded from his recent new book, *The Broken Heart: The Medical Consequences of Loneliness.* "Loneliness is not only pushing our culture to the breaking point," he says, "it is pushing our physical health to the breaking point."

The consequences for refusing to obey God are grim. Poet W. H. Auden said it dramatically: "We must love one another or die."

Not all marriages can be salvaged, of course. I would be foolish to suggest such an impossibility, but I do encourage you to "exhaust every resource you can before you settle for a split. While every marriage will not be saved, nothing is lost by trying again."[5]

"One reason for our lack of love for our loved ones," Karen Mains suggests, "is that through the years we have come to concentrate on what is bad in another. The enlarging machine in our minds blows the negative all out of proportion."[6]

The first step in trying to restore an ailing marriage is to *gain perspective* and to deal with this emphasis on the negative. Hope MacDonald uses a helpful exercise in her speaking seminars. These exercises work for healthy marriages as well:

1. Make a list of your mate's *good* qualities—mental, physical, and spiritual.

2. Now list all the things you have tried to change in your mate.
3. Compare this list with the first one.
4. Ask God to show you what is really important.
5. Tell your mate one nice thing about himself (herself) every day this week.

This is only a start, but it's a good one. And since you have to start somewhere, this is a logical place. When your attitude begins to change, then you are not so critical.

So the second step is to *stop criticizing*. Finding fault is a bad habit that must be broken just like any other habit. For a while it takes conscious effort every time we catch ourselves finding fault. Then we must confess the sin (1 John 1:9), receive forgiveness and cleansing, and start again with a clean slate. If we set our will, that by the grace of God we're going to obey Him and reflect a loving heart at all times, we will get the victory.

Early in the healing process we must *forgive*. It probably will take many forgiving sessions before our hearts are pure in this respect, but God never commanded us to do anything He would not give power to accomplish. It doesn't matter if we *feel* like forgiving or not. The question is, Are we going to obey God? If so, then it's a matter of the will, not feeling. Frankly, I never *feel* like forgiving someone when I am offended. If I waited until I felt like it, I'd *never* obey God. Sometimes I have to say to God, "I'm going to obey You if it kills me." The wounds inflicted on me are often so deep that I think it will kill me, but God so wondrously heals those wounds and binds up my broken heart that the joy afterward cannot be described. God knows that if we don't forgive one another, we end up destroying ourselves—especially in marriage. "The results of forgiveness," writes Karen Mains, "are well worth the struggle of yanking our wills to the painful point of obedience. Finding the possible in the impossible is always a thrill."[7]

What about those marriages that cannot be salvaged,

however? Some have made wrong choices or are innocent victims of another's choice. Perhaps the term "innocent" is slightly inaccurate, for where problems exist between two people, neither can claim absolute innocence. But is there no hope for the lonely sufferer of a broken marriage, whatever the cause?

Certainly! There is always hope, help, and healing when we look to God, the Friend of the friendless. There is always forgiveness and wholeness available. God delights in remaking broken lives, even as Jeremiah's potter, who took the marred vessel and formed it into another vessel, "shaping it as seemed best to him" (Jer. 18:4 NIV). Before this can happen, though, the vessel has to yield to the potter's hand, and loneliness can be the very instrument used of God to bring this about.

Laurie was an example of God's healing, restoring power. Her first marriage, begun in disobedience to parents and an elopement before she was seventeen, seemed destined from the beginning for failure. After four years of hanging on, trying to make the marriage work, the inevitable happened. By the time she walked away, there was nothing left of the union, and she experienced no remorse, no guilt —only relief to be out of the impossible situation.

She was three months pregnant when the marriage ended, but even that didn't matter. She had her baby alone and set out to raise him alone. Musically gifted, she had no trouble finding a good paying job in a night club, and life was filled with gaiety, laughter, people, parties, and good times. For a few years. After a while, the glitter wore off and loneliness crept in. Only slightly, at first. But it grew. And it grew. Finally, after five years she was literally submerged in self-pity and buried in loneliness.

It was the loneliness, however, that drove her to her solution. All other relationships had crumbled and failed, so she was forced to seek the God of her childhood, finding new life and new hope in Jesus Christ. The transformation that followed was nothing short of a miracle, but it took the giant of loneliness to bring it about.

I like happy endings, don't you? This story has such a happy ending that I must share it with you. Another miracle of God occurred to bring two lonely people together who had never heard of each other and who lived 2,500 miles apart. Loneliness had driven Bob, whom I mentioned earlier, to an unconditional surrender to his Lord. Loneliness forced Laurie to find a personal relationship with the Savior she somehow missed as a child. When the two of them separately yielded their entire lives to God, He was ready to bring them together—two very marred vessels—and make a new vessel as seemed good to Him. And that new vessel is pouring forth a new song of praise to the divine Potter in a music ministry that blesses the hearts of thousands.

Let me give you some practical advice if you belong to the great and growing company of the "formerly married." As a Christian, you are undoubtedly experiencing guilt, a sense of failure, low self-esteem, and a feeling of being unloved. "Whether you are just beginning to lose your grip on your marriage, or if it has already slipped through your fingers, you can't help feeling unloved . . . and perhaps even unlovable."[8] The emotional pressure of these problems drives many a divorced person prematurely into another marriage before such a decision can be adequately handled. It takes a long time to heal after the radical surgery of divorce, so give it time.

Also, begin to work with God according to His laws, and healing will occur more quickly and completely. "Go to God. Pour out your pain and your anger. As simply, as directly as you can, tell Him what you are feeling. Let it all out. He won't be surprised or shocked."[9]

Since we are all separate persons with no two of us alike in the world, formulas don't operate the same for everyone. The following suggestions toward healing and wholeness for the divorced Christian are merely that—suggestions.

1. Since guilt is a common response to divorce, ask God's forgiveness. Confess any sin He brings to your mind, and then believe you are forgiven once for all.

2. Surrender the rest of your life to God, no matter how shattered you feel. Accept God's unconditional love.

3. Stop living for the sole purpose of finding another mate. If God wants you to have one, He will arrange it. Many conditions are worse than singleness. A bad marriage, for instance.

4. Expand your mental horizons. Take a course in a subject you've always wanted to know more about, or do something you didn't have time to do when married.

5. Find a church where you can be comfortable, preferably with a ministry to the divorced, and become actively involved. Don't become spiritually isolated.

6. Seek Christian counseling if you feel the need for it. Take advantage of any Christian divorce recovery programs available in your locality.

Can God heal the lonely and brokenhearted? Find out for yourself. He is waiting to enter your heart, to fill the lonely void, and to be the Friend you need.

10

What About My Family?

Is the family unit in America a diminishing reality? No one can deny that the family is deteriorating due to increased outside pressures, divorce, women exchanging the home for salaried jobs, abortion, and all the forces at work undermining the importance of the family. Christian families are not exempt from these influences, and if the family is to survive, I believe it will be because God-fearing people refuse to let the world dictate its standards to them.

While I fully recognize the necessity of a strong family unit, I find myself in conflicting positions because of my calling to the ministry. How does a traveling evangelist, or any Christian worker for that matter, meet the needs of a family and his ministry at the same time?

Struggling with these considerations and trying to balance the growing demands of both place me in a lonely position much of the time. "Sometimes the man of faith feels his aloneness when those of the church, perhaps, charge him falsely with neglecting his family. Sometimes the uncertainty of whether the 'calling is really sure' can plague the mind and heart. Sometimes the sense of whether anyone really cares (that someone is putting family, houses and lands behind to carry the cause of Christ) can bring a sense of loneliness."[1]

In striving to reach a balance, I have failed my wife and family many times. Not because I have placed my ministry above my family, but often because I haven't known exactly what to do. An illustration of my frequent quandary in such matters occurred at the time our third daughter was born.

My room in Lansing, Michigan, was buzzing with reporters and photographers, and we were in the midst of an important press conference preceding a well-publicized city-wide crusade. The telephone rang.

"Nicky," Gloria's frightened voice pleaded, "please come home right away. I need you so badly."

Cupping my hand over the mouthpiece and turning my back to the news-hungry press representatives lest they hear and suspect domestic problems in the life of "God's man of faith and power," I hoarsely whispered, "Gloria, I am in the middle of an important press conference. I have all these reporters here in my room. *I can't* come home."

"But, Nicky," she persisted, "they have taken our baby into surgery, and the doctors don't know if she'll live. I'm not sure I can get through this without you. *Please* come."

"Gloria, honey, I wish I *could,* but can't you see, there's no way. The crusade opens tonight and thousands of people will be coming. We can't cancel—it's too late to notify the public."

The room became disturbingly quiet, so I hung up the phone quickly without another word, my heart heavy with guilt and torn by responsibilities. Before turning to face the waiting reporters, I forced a superficial smile. Only God could see me through this crisis, I knew. And what of Gloria? I breathed a quick prayer for her and our new baby.

Our third child, Nicole, had arrived early. Before leaving for this crusade, I questioned the doctor, who assured me that the baby would not be born for at least another two weeks. Had I mistrusted the doctor's judgment, I would have canceled the crusade. Instead, I boarded a plane persuading myself all would be well at home. A strange foreboding undermined my usual calm, however, and it wasn't many hours before that subconscious premonition (or was it a divine forewarning that I ignored?) became reality, and the baby was born.

Except for Hope, a very young woman on my staff, Gloria was all alone when her labor began. They had gone for a walk about 7:00, and by 11:30 that night hard labor set in. Hope had no choice but to drive Gloria to the hospital and leave the other little children alone sleeping. The labor pains became so intense that Gloria laid herself down on the tiny Volkswagen seat as best she could. What a pair they must have been: Gloria writhing in agony trying to keep the baby from being delivered in that little Beetle, and Hope scared to death as she drove. They made it just in time.

Back in that Fresno hospital, another facet of the mysterious drama was unfolding, I later learned. Gloria lay in the hospital bed the morning after Nicole's birth wondering why she hadn't seen the baby. *Surely they didn't bring her in when I was half-conscious, and I can't remember that I saw her,* she reflected. She rang the nurse on duty and inquired about her baby.

"Oh, the baby's just fine. You'll be seeing her soon," she said as she turned quickly and left the room.

Something is wrong, I know it is, Gloria intuitively felt. As the day wore on and not a soul came near her room, her suspicions increased. She could pry nothing from the nurses, who continued to assure her that Nicole was fine, but they always failed to bring her to Gloria's room. Finally, by evening, our children's trusted pediatrician made a routine newborn check in the nursery and stopped by Gloria's room on the way out.

"Gloria," Dr. Shakerian gently said, "I hope you'll be brave, because I have bad news for you. Your baby is extremely sick, and unless we take her immediately to Children's Hospital for emergency surgery, she can't possibly live."

Stunned, Gloria inquired as to the nature of the baby's problem.

"She was born with a large hole in her diaphragm, and her vital organs have squeezed through the hole up into her chest," the doctor patiently explained. "Only about one baby in 100,000 lives when born with this condition," he slowly added.

Nicole was transported promptly to Children's Hospital and whisked away in preparation for the life-and-death procedure.

"Where is your husband?" the attending nurse asked Gloria.

"Out of town," she murmured, making no attempt to explain.

"You must sign a release," the businesslike voice continued.

Gloria later told me, "Nicky, my hand was moving, but I didn't feel a thing inside or out. I was numb. I couldn't think. The responsibility I faced was so awesome—a tiny life that I had carried within my body for almost a year was hanging in the balance, and I had no one to lean on. Even God seemed at a distance, and I was almost too weak to pray anyway."

"Were you mad at me, Gloria?" I pressed her further, even though I had canceled the rest of my crusade and flown to her side.

"Both mad and hurt," she confessed. "You had hung up on me, and I wasn't able to explain further how weak I was, how delicate the surgery, or how alone and afraid I felt." Then she said emphatically, "I know you are a God-called man, Nicky, and I am as committed to this ministry as you are—but this is ridiculous. Surely family emergencies take precedence over everything else. Or do they?"

"Gloria, honey, I've told you how sorry I am," I repeated, "but it's hard always to know what I'm supposed to do."

"But you didn't have to hang up on me, Nicky. I couldn't even discuss my crisis with the only person in all the world who could help me. And I didn't dare call back."

I knew Gloria was right, but I also knew that no one except the Lord really understood what I was going through, and my predicament couldn't be easily solved—if at all. Gloria and I together had prayed for God's blessing on my new ministry. Now that it had come, the demands far exceeded the ability of one man to meet them. Traveling was a necessity, and while it might have appeared all glamour to be the featured attraction of TV and radio interviews, newspapers and billboards that plastered my picture everywhere, and thousands attending city-wide crusades, there was another side of it, too. A hidden side which, again, no one but the Lord and I knew.

"Perhaps it is true that some men, in the name of God and the faith, thrive on jet lag and find that traveling is their 'life call'."[2] But for me, traveling in airplanes, haggling at ticket counters, recovering lost baggage, sitting hours exhausted in airports in the middle of the night, riding half asleep in taxis to impersonal hotels, sleeping in a variety of beds, and staring at four bleak walls while wishing to be in my own home with my own wife and my own children, is not my idea of glamour. The loneliness that sets in when I am away from my family for long periods becomes acute.

As I travel across this country and throughout the world, I am constantly overwhelmed by the staggering number of people who suffer from this malady of loneliness. Because of my lifelong journey of rejection and aloneness, I am able to relate deeply. What if they do not, or cannot, call on the Lord for help? Too many people fit into the category of lonely people and find it so easy to turn to alcohol, or drugs, or sex, or suicide. Still others seek to fill the void with ceaseless activity or people. Lots of people. Countless millions waste their lives in the grip of loneliness and confusion without the slightest notion that there is an escape.

I have learned to recognize this condition in those who come to me for help. Usually they do not express their problem as loneliness. Most of the time I suspect they don't even know it. When they begin to describe other symptoms, and I sense the real problem and begin to touch on it and minister to this need, a tearful recognition and assent often follows. Then we are at the heart of the matter.

I remind them, first of all, that God is there, available for help. Somehow, they have lost sight of that fact. Or, they know it intellectually, but can't translate the knowledge into their experience.

"I will never leave thee, nor forsake thee," Jesus said, "so that we may boldly say, The Lord is my helper, and I will not fear . . ." (Heb. 13:5).

Don't be afraid to call on God, I insist. He *wants* us to do this. He said that we are to come "boldly unto the throne of grace, that we may obtain mercy, and find grace to help in time of need" (Heb. 4:16). And when we do, He will come and have fellowship with our spirit. He will renew our faith. Remember that He is the greatest Friend we have, one who "sticks closer than a brother" (Prov. 18:24).

When I am counseling lonely people, I am glad I can say, "I know just how you feel. I experience the same thing, especially when I travel, and just knowing that God is my best Friend helps immensely. I deal with loneliness through Christ, not on my own strength."

I tell my counselees that when loneliness and depression set in, they should not listen to their voices. They will try to convince us that we are failures, that we should give up. *Maybe God doesn't really care after all,* that voice whispers, *so go ahead, give in to that weakness. It doesn't matter. You really blew it—look at this mess—just forget it.*

Don't listen to that voice of defeat. Instead, listen to the sweet voice of the Good Shepherd, the strong voice of the One who wants to come and minister to you in those moments when you need Him most. *He is there,* waiting for you to open your heart to Him, to give Him those hurts and negative feelings of rejection. He will renew you.

Although I've just outlined some of my own problems in striving for an equitable solution to the family/work issue, I realize that my work is not typical of most husbands and fathers. Yet no man who shoulders responsibility in his work escapes many of the same considerations that I face. My particular calling involves the kind of responsibility that "knows" no definite working hours. My work is not taken up and laid down at the blowing of a whistle, nor is it governed by a time clock. Margaret Wood aptly described this life when she said that "those who bear it feel its burden heaviest in wakeful night hours when their more carefree fellows are at rest."[3]

The "eight-to-five" businessman finds his adjustments to family living different from mine; still, we all face a number of similar considerations and adjustments. Who would deny that families can be very lonely in spite of shared experiences in a common dwelling place? Parents especially need to be aware of this and try to do something about it. Recognizing ahead of time a few of the common trouble spots and facing them together can eliminate much of the loneliness families experience.

Assuming that both parents are Christians and moving in the same direction, one of the most important bits of advice they need to heed is *work together.* It seems almost unnecessary to emphasize this, but recognize it or not, many couples are heading in different directions to the confusion of their children. No one is communicating with anyone. Each is going a separate way, thinking separate thoughts, making separate decisions, and longing for a closer relationship with family members.

Parents, begin to change this pattern. Start talking. To

each other. To your children. Turn loose those bottled-up thoughts and put them into words. You may have to hang up the telephone or turn off the television. But *you* are the parents, and this is your responsibility.

Almost any communication is better than none. Where problems exist, call the family together, and let the words fly. Be open. You may have to function as an umpire, father or mother, but remember, you are the adults. Keep your goal in mind. A little temporary disagreement is worth clarifying the issues that keep the family from experiencing unity.

Setting family priorities is one of the most difficult objectives to achieve. Finally, after all these years, I am learning to say no and schedule quality and quantity time with my family. It's not easy. At first I found myself present in body only with my mind deeply engrossed in making new plans and with solving the problems of my work. As Gloria and I are working together to set everything else aside and enter the world of our children, we are enjoying it more. Probably the greatest reward is that the children are enjoying it too, and are counting our time together as a family their top priority.

Family worship can be a creative force to bind together each member and drive away the lonelies. It's worth every effort to maintain regularity. Variety in method serves to sustain interest and encourage participation on the part of each family person. Some of the different approaches could include:

1. Read from a daily devotional book and allow comments afterward.
2. Using a modern language Bible, read a consecutive portion each day. Lead into discussion by posing provocative questions.
3. Select relevant subjects, assign a related Scripture to each person to read and explain.
4. Take turns one day a week by allowing each family member to prepare and lead the devotional.

5. Pass out Scripture (Daily Manna-type) to each person to read and explain what it means personally and how to apply the truth in everyday life.

These are only a few suggestions, but it is wise to change your routine often to keep the children stimulated and interested. Teach them conversational prayer, open-type discussion, and spontaneity, and incorporate singing of hymns and choruses as a regular part of your worship. Select the time of day that fits your schedule, and maintain it if you have to take it by force. And you may have to, because your adversary, the devil, is seeking to destroy family unity.

Where are the family trouble spots, moms and dads? They vary with each individual situation, of course, but let's mention a few.

Discipline of children: Any couple who has not disagreed often and violently here does not have children yet. Or they're still in the crib. This is the hot spot of many a marriage, and probably the most damaging to the kids. If the parents put up a united front regardless of personal feelings, the children learn to respect authority and will obey. They cannot assail the inpregnable wall of agreed parental authority, but if they detect even the slightest crack, they will pit one against another until the wall comes tumbling down.

Just this past week a distraught father sought my counsel. "What can I do with my fifteen-year-old son?" he begged. "He defies me on every hand, ridicules me, rebels at every suggestion, and is pressing me to let him get an apartment with a friend so he can do as he pleases. I'm afraid I've been too lenient for too long, and I don't know what to do with him now. He simply pays no attention to me and treats me as if I am the stupidest person alive."

"What about your wife?" I queried. "Has she been overindulgent and lax, also?"

"Heavens, no. She has been unreasonably strict, and I've had to try to counterbalance her senseless demands on the children."

After further conversation, I concluded that it was, indeed, too late for the fifteen-year-old. The leniency of the father or the strictness of the mother were not the conclusive factors. Had both the parents stood together at one extreme or the other, the boy might have had a chance.

Finances: This is reputed to be at the top of the list of reasons for divorce. While I will not take time to dispute or defend that statement, I wish merely to acknowledge the importance of reaching a workable solution in this explosive area of family life. "Most financial problems occur in the spending area," writes Don Meredith. I would highly recommend his book, *Becoming One,* for an in-depth treatment of marriage and family problems. Let me share with you his helpful chart on the matter of expenditures and questions you might ask yourself:

Question	Scripture
1. Is my spending motivated by the love of things or love toward others?	1 Timothy 6:9 1 John 2:15
2. Has God already led me to meet a need with this money?	2 Corinthians 8:14 Proverbs 3:9–10
3. Do I have a doubt about it?	Romans 14:23
4. Have I given God an opportunity to supply it?	Psalm 37:5 Proverbs 10:3
5. Is it a good investment?	Proverbs 20:14
6. Does it put me in debt?	Proverbs 22:7
7. Will it be meaningful to my family?	1 Timothy 5:8 and 1 Timothy 3:4

"Each of these factors should be balanced against all others in making a decision. Wise counsel from another person helps. A couple who keeps tight control over their purchases should have little trouble keeping God's perspective."[4]

In-laws: There is much to be said in resolving these conflicts, but the two simplest words of advice I can give are straight from the Scriptures:

> *Leave and cleave*
> *Don't criticize*

These two injunctions when wholeheartedly applied in obedience to God can straighten out the worst in-law messes ever to exist. Try it.

One of the most valuable ingredients for family togetherness and enjoyment is simply to *accept one another* as God's creative masterpieces. Of course, we're all different. If we weren't, some of us would be duplications and unnecessary. It's good to keep in mind that no one is perfect —especially me! Loving, unconditional acceptance of your spouse can heal many a wounded spirit.

The following rules for happy marriage can give yours a brand new start and revitalize family relationships:

1. Never both be angry at the same time.
2. Never yell at each other unless the house is on fire.
3. If one of you *has* to win an argument, let it be your mate.
4. If you have to criticize, do it lovingly.
5. Never bring up mistakes of the past.
6. Neglect the whole world rather than each other.
7. Never go to sleep with an argument unsettled.
8. At least once every day try to say one kind or complimentary thing to your life's partner.
9. When you have done something wrong, be ready to admit it and ask for forgiveness.
10. It takes two to make a quarrel, and the one in the wrong is the one who does the most talking.

11

All Those Lonely People— Why Are So Many in Church?

Church is the happiest place on earth. Once you enter its portals, you can leave your worries and cares behind. Its members love each other with undying devotion, they are ready to forgive and forget at a moment's notice, they always think the best of each other, always speak well of one another, and stick together like glue. There is no such thing as loneliness, lovelessness, or snobbery. It's like heaven on earth.

If the above statement were true, eager mobs would be tearing down church doors trying to get in, lost people would be asking, "What must I do to be saved?" and God's kingdom soon would be established on earth. Church members like to pretend something of this sort is true of their church and are reluctant to face the discouraging facts. It becomes very uncomfortable if a member happens to let his smiling mask slip to reveal hurt, humiliation, loneliness, or discontent. Surely that is not evidence of spirituality. We must live up to our high standards, you know, or people might criticize us.

What has happened in the intervening years between

now and the early New Testament church when it could be said by an observer, "Behold, how they love one another"? Jesus Himself told us how we could recognize His followers when He said: "Your strong love for each other will prove to the world that you are my disciples" (John 13:35 LB). Once Jesus asked the question, "When the Son of Man comes, will he find *faith* on the earth?" (Luke 18:9 NIV). Perhaps He should have added "love."

This is not to generalize and leave the impression that all churches are devoid of love and compassion. Such a statement would be grossly unfair and untrue. Certainly there are notable exceptions, and the world is blessed by them. However, I am hearing more often these days the same lament wherever I travel. It is like a song in which only the verses change, never the tune. Pastors, evangelists, and lay Christian people alike are singing the song in a minor key and wondering where they can go to find genuine love and acceptance. Too often churches are torn apart by bickering, divisiveness, competition, and pettiness. Jesus' final plea to His beloved followers before He left the earth to go to His heavenly Father, ". . . go and make disciples of all nations . . . teaching them to observe everything I have commanded you," finds little enactment due to the magnitude of the local church's internal problems.

"The church corporate," writes Karen Mains, "that household of the living God, has too often formed itself into a series of fortified camps, entrenched not against the enemy without, but against the enemy within. Cold, silent wars or outright major offensives—it doesn't matter which, hostilities are occurring. Word bombardments are being unleashed. Slaughter is havocking the board meeting. Bloodshed is launched in the women's sewing circle."[1]

Some of the loneliest people I find in churches are the ministers and their staff. Lonelier still are their wives. Oh, they are busy—preaching, teaching Bible classes, visiting the "sick, wounded, and afflicted," counseling, running to socials and church dinners. People are friendly enough—in the church, that is—but there is really no one to whom they can say, "Hey, I wasn't born a preacher. I'm a real person just like you. I hurt inside. I worry about my kids. I hardly ever have enough money to go around, and I often long for things I don't have. I get lonely, too, and I get tired of always smiling and hiding the fact that I am human just like you are."

The honest but sad truth is that most Christians do not want their pastors, evangelists, or other Christian leaders to be human. It's all right for them to show weakness or to have needs, but the man or woman of God must be above this. We place them on an impossible pedestal, maintain a cruel distance from them lest we catch a glimpse of their humanity. We shake our heads and loudly denounce them if they chance to slip and fall. No wonder so many are slipping and falling these days, for after spending years selflessly giving their lives to others, there are no hands that reach out to lift them up. They only throw stones.

Somehow we have lost sight of what the apostle Paul tried to explain when he said, ". . . we have this treasure in earthen vessels, that the excellency of the power may be of God, and not of us" (2 Cor. 4:7). Indeed, all Christians possess the treasure of the glory of God living within, and it is this indwelling treasure that produces the power we need in order to live godly lives. When we see the treasure shining brightly in our spiritual leaders, we praise God and shout "Hallelujah!" But if we happen to catch sight of the earthen vessel, we turn away in disappointment and say, "I don't understand. What has happened? If that's Christianity, I don't need it." Often we spend so much time looking at the earthen vessel we miss the brilliance of the treasure.

A minister friend of mine who pastored a church for several years, faithfully seeing it through ups and downs and in betweens, confided in me recently. He said, "You know, Nicky, I gave everything I had to that church during those years. God knows I neglected my family, but what do you do with the multiplied demands constantly pressing you? There were always sick people, my appointment book bulged with troubled souls needing counseling, and my phone rang incessantly so that I could hardly give myself to prayer and the study of God's Word. If I took a day off, there was no rest unless I left town. Then I was often criticized if someone happened to die or needed me on that day.

"But I accepted all of this as part of what I signed up for when I gave my life to God's service. I did not complain. Neither did my family, praise the Lord. A funny thing happened, though. When it came my turn, and I had to resign because of illness, the sick and troubled hands I held during those years did not reach out for mine. I faced my trial all alone. Where were all those people who gratefully said, 'I couldn't have made it without you, Pastor'? Do they suppose I don't need a loving touch, an encouraging word, concrete evidence that somebody cares? Maybe they think I am so spiritual that they could offer little comfort at a time like this."

An isolated example? You better not believe it! If you do, you're not in touch with reality in the life of God-called servants. There are many compensations, and most of us would not trade our privileged position for all the friends, money, excitement, or possessions this world may offer. On the other hand, I cannot be blind to the fact that men are leaving the ministry in record numbers. Undoubtedly some of them were not truly called of God. But I have talked to many who were, and they are saying, "It's just not worth it. Your hands are tied in the average church, and a man can't do what he was called to do—there's just too much internal strife, divisiveness, pressure, and politics. I've had it!"

What about the average church attender who quietly files into the pew, smiles at a few familiar faces but never really knows the person behind the smile, who earnestly seeks to grow as a Christian. "If you're lonely," everyone keeps advising, "find yourself a good church and be faithful. That's the place to make friends." So you do it. How long does it take to make friends and get over the loneliness? You've been in that same church for nearly two years, and you still haven't made it with the "in" crowd.

The "in" crowd? That's an interesting observation. There must be "ins" and "outs" then. Maybe you're different, you surmise, and don't quite fit with the "ins." Maybe you aren't friendly enough, or you are too sensitive. Everyone looks so content and so spiritual, as if they don't have the problems you're struggling with.

As I listen to hurting people while counseling during my crusades, and when I turn to my letter file, I find perpetual evidence that our churches are filled with lonely, searching souls. Listen to a part of a letter from a young husband whose wife left with their two children to live with another man:

> The more I try, the worse it gets. I just don't know what to do—I really don't. Loneliness is killing me. So why not end it all. I just can't take it anymore.

> When I was playing my guitar or the piano in church, the people looked at me as if they wished I would leave. So I did. I guess I just didn't have it, because I went back on Jesus. Things got out of hand, and I just couldn't go on. I really wanted to live for Jesus. I really did.

Here's another letter—a pathetic plea from an eighteen-year-old boy trying to make it against countless odds:

> I was at your crusade in St. Louis. I saw so much that I wanted. I'm so confused and filled with hate, bitterness, and loneliness. I've got troubles all around me. My father said he hates me, and I hate him. I heard my mother tell my sister that I would never make anything

of my life, and she was right. I dropped out of school. I can't find a job, and they really can't afford me living at home.

I go to church all the time, and I want to do right, but there's something wrong with me. I just want to lie down and die. I've caused so much trouble and have hurt so many people. I just want to die.

My friend Laurie, whom I mentioned earlier, had a tough struggle when she decided to bury her past life of sin and live for Jesus. "Every time I tried to get up," she recalls, "there was the foot of another Christian on my neck, daring me to move. I think I understood the statement that the church is the only army that shoots its wounded instead of nursing them back to health."

Are we better than Jesus? The Bible tells us that He went out of His way to associate with sinners. Naturally, the self-righteous religious leaders of His day didn't understand. They asked Jesus' disciples, "Why does your teacher associate with men like that?" Jesus Himself answered them directly, "Because people who are well don't need a doctor! It's the sick people who do. . . . I have come to urge sinners, not the self-righteous, back to God" (Matt. 9:11–13 LB).

Perhaps a closer look at the first-century believers will clear our vision and remind us what the church is all about, and why there are such glaring differences in today's version. First of all, Jesus had prayed for His followers to be "one," and unity of heart and soul characterized those early groups. They seemed to understand the lordship of Jesus Christ in a way we have missed, and they took literally the command, "And whatever you do, whether in word or deed, do it all in the name of the Lord Jesus . . ." (Col. 3:17 NIV). Their entire purpose for living was to please the Savior who died for them and who called them out of darkness into light.

"All the believers were one in heart and mind. No one claimed that any of his possessions was his own, but they shared everything they had. . . . There were no needy persons among them" (Acts 4:32, 34 NIV).

I was speaking with a Korean man, Hai Wan Suh, who had lived all his life in Seoul, Korea, but who had recently moved with his family to the United States and was now a pastor of Korean immigrants in Colorado Springs. He was laughing as he was telling me, "Moving is such hard work. First we moved into an apartment, and I carried everything *up* three flights of stairs. Then we bought a house, and I carried everything *down* three flights of stairs. I never realized how difficult it is to move. In Korea, you know, everybody comes to help and it doesn't seem so hard."

I laughed with him, but secretly I felt ashamed that this frail, new citizen of my country should be introduced to our "Christian love and compassion" so quickly, and I wondered if those stalwart first-century believers would have left my Korean friends to struggle alone up and down those flights of stairs. "There were no needy persons among them," it says.

Those early believers met together often, not just when it was convenient, and their fellowship was deep and intimate. They were concerned about each other, greeted each other with "a holy kiss," and often wept when they were separated.

Perhaps the chief ingredient providing the missing key to the mystery of the two churches, then and now, is persecution. Whether we like to consider it or not, a persecuted church or believer either turns his heels and runs, or begins to stand and be counted. Suffering draws people together in a mutual bond of love and protectiveness. Priorities automatically fall into place, and the difference between important and non-important pursuits becomes remarkably clear. The apostle Peter, one of the chief spokesmen for the early church, knew what he was talking about when he said, "He that has suffered in the flesh has ceased from sin" (1 Peter 4:1).

Have you ever observed the startling transition that takes place in a person who has had a heart attack or has cancer? Each day becomes the most precious commodity he possesses, and since he may not have time to accomplish all he'd hoped to, excess activities and people drop off like flies in November. You don't have to beg that person to attend church. The Lord becomes so precious, and he tries to make up for wasted time. He pays more attention to his family and less to mere friends and acquaintances. In an exceedingly brief time, he becomes what he knew he should have been all along.

I am not saying the church needs persecution. If it comes, however—and many prophetic scholars are saying it most certainly will—the result will be a purified church. I believe we would swiftly return to scriptural principles and practices, and the fervor and flavor of the early church would be evidenced again.

Meanwhile, where can we find in our community the kind of Christian fellowship and friendship we need to help us through these trying days? Shall we leave our troubled church and seek other groups? Not necessarily, for the vast majority of churches across our land report a similar state of decline, so it might be the course of wisdom to begin closer even than the church by looking within our own heart.

A woman I know who was experiencing great problems finding Christian friends, and who was suffering from loneliness and a constant feeling of rejection, decided her need might be spiritual. She began to spend more time studying the Bible and praying. She also started to attend all the services in her church, including the midweek prayer service. Still her problem persisted, and she felt as lonely as ever.

Finally, she went to her pastor and tearfully poured out her unhappy state. The advice he gave her was the wisdom of Solomon. He said, "In whatever area you need help, give that same help to someone else. In so doing, you will find the help you are seeking."

As she took her eyes off herself and began to notice other lonely people, she realized that she had been trying to break into the "in" groups and hadn't even noticed how many others remained outside that closed circle. Prayerfully selecting just one person at first, she reached out warmly. It wasn't hard, and the response was immediate. Her satisfaction at being needed in the life of another was so great that she reached out to one more lonely person. After a few months, it dawned on my friend that without even realizing what had taken place, she had begun a ministry, and before long, a happy little group of "ins" clustered about her. The only difference between the two "in" groups was that she determined her circle would always be open and would be seeking to minister to other lonely "outs."

One of the most inspiring people I know is a young woman who at thirty-two has chosen to remain single in obedience to God. She is taking the Christian world by storm and is saying wherever she goes, "I'm out to change my world!" Ann Kiemel is a prolific writer and travels probably hundreds of thousands of miles each year telling people why she loves the word "impossible." And I believe she does. Her life is daily proof of it.

When you hear Ann Kiemel speak, you realize she is not gifted, or eloquent, or necessarily dynamic. In fact, she comes through as rather shy, retiring, and unpretentious. After listening awhile, though, you know she means what she says. She is in constant demand as a speaker at major Christian functions, and I know from experience that she must return to her Boston apartment weary and spent. In spite of that, she reportedly sets aside one entire day of each week to minister to her neighbors. It may be simply a plate of warm cookies straight from the oven, or a gift for the new baby, or a visit with a lonely housewife. She designs her offerings to meet specific needs.

Ann Kiemel is not discouraged because she is only one person and can do so little compared to the world's immense spiritual poverty. Quite the contrary. "I am only one person," she smiles as she speaks, "but I am one." If we as Christians purposed in our hearts to change our little sphere of environment, be it home or church or world, we could do it!

If you are like the friend I mentioned earlier who was having difficulty finding Christian friends and who suffered greatly from loneliness, it might be wise to begin where she did—before the Lord. Then ask yourself a few questions like the following:

Are you overtly friendly, reaching out to others and speaking first if necessary?

Do you show an interest in the lives and problems of others?

Are you a good listener, or do you always like to talk about yourself?

Are you supersensitive, often imagining that people avoid you?

Have you stopped trying to be friendly because of previous experiences of rejection?

You may not be able to change your whole church, but you can change the course of your personal life. In the process, however, you may be surprised to find that you initiated a chain reaction.

12

How Not to Be Lonely

"Loneliness is the single experience most common to all of us, yet is also the most misunderstood."[1] Loneliness is universal. Every person alive experiences it to some measure, because no one can crawl inside another human being to see what's really there. For that reason, we will always be misunderstood to a certain degree. We will always be somewhat rejected. We will always feel a bit like an outsider, no matter what our circumstances might be.

Loneliness, you see, is not caused by our circumstances. We can be in the midst of a happy crowd, the life of a party, and still be lonely within. *Loneliness is a state of mind,* not a set of circumstances. "At the heart of the experience of loneliness is the sense of isolation and separation. It may include the sense of being left out, of being rejected, of being estranged, of not being understood, of being abandoned. Loneliness involves the FEELING that there is no one and no thing responsive to our deep hunger for support and caring."[2]

As we conclude our discussion of loneliness, we need to understand the differences between aloneness, solitude, and loneliness. "Our greatest mistake is in not distinguishing between 'aloneness' and 'loneliness'," insists Harvey Potthoff.

Aloneness is a state of being physically separated from other people. There are times in our lives beyond our control, when the company of family, friends, or other persons is missing. We cannot reach out and touch one another.

However, because we are alone, it does not necessarily mean we are lonely. We simply take these times in stride and recognize that life cannot always be filled with people. "Our periods of aloneness, if simply allowed to happen, to be experienced by ourselves, can be among the most rewarding of our lives. It is possible to be alone and not lonely."[3]

Often it is a relief to be alone. We accomplish more, we can think more clearly without the need to talk, and the absence of noise or confusion is soothing to the nerves. Being frequently alone is positive, constructive, and necessary for everyone. "Allowing ourselves to accept our aloneness experiences serves ultimately to bring out our best possibilities. It can give us time to evaluate our goals, the quality of our work, values, and faith, and can lead us to new appreciation of our husbands and wives, friends, or God."[4]

> For God alone my soul waits in silence; from him comes my salvation. He only is my rock and my salvation, my fortress; I shall not be greatly moved (Ps. 62:1–2 RSV).

Solitude is the act of intentionally withdrawing from others for the purpose of being alone. Paul Tillich said that "loneliness can be conquered only by those who can bear solitude." This is the time when we are refreshed spiritually, restored emotionally, and regain mental balance. Solitude is essential for maintaining wholeness and developing spiritual depth.

Solitude can be renewing and creative. "Sometimes we choose to be alone in order to find ourselves and to get things put together. Most of us need times of solitude."[5]

Jesus Himself needed these times of solitude with His heavenly Father. Matthew 14:23 says, "And after he had dismissed the crowds, he went on the mountain *by himself* to pray. When evening came, he was there alone" (RSV).

The superficiality that characterizes the modern Christian is due largely to the lack of solitude. We rush here and there to evangelistic meetings, concerts, rallies, Bible studies, crusades, retreats, conferences, and services of every description thinking we are "filling our cup"—and all the while wondering why we feel so empty. The trouble is that we are merely taking second hand what another person has received directly from God during hours of solitude, prayer, meditation, and the personal study of God's Word. We could have the same direct blessing, but we're too busy with our running around.

Vance Havner once said something like this: "If we don't come apart to be with God, we'll come apart." Too many of us are experiencing that second "coming apart."

Loneliness dealt with creatively yields power. "Much can be done by way of weaving the pain of loneliness into a pattern of meaningful and productive living. This process involves the creative use of solitude."[6] It is possible to experience solitude without suffering loneliness in the slightest degree. Indeed, "we have within us the capacity to turn our loneliness into solitude, our strangeness into holiness."[7]

Finally, *loneliness* is neither aloneness nor solitude. It is a feeling of being alienated, or cut off, or rejected by others.

The basic insecurity that produces loneliness is the result of depending on people to produce the feeling of being needed and loved. Without this feeling, we experience deep inner loneliness.

Tanner speaks of the "disease of loneliness." He points out that "the person who says 'I am never lonely' either does not understand the meaning of the word or is fooling himself. Loneliness is something we all have to deal with at one time or another in our lives."[8]

Let's face it. To be alive is to experience the pain of loneliness. "Some measure of loneliness seems to be part of the price tag of being human," reminds Potthoff.[9] Although we cannot always change our circumstances that produce loneliness, we can do something about our responses to our circumstances.

You will notice my emphasis on feeling. That's exactly what loneliness is, and the sooner we recognize this fact, the sooner we can deal with it and overcome its destructive tendencies. The feeling of loneliness has driven multitudes to deadly introspection, depression, alcoholism, drugs, suicide, and many other tragic excesses.

"If loneliness is the FEELING of not being meaningfully related, it is good news to know that there are some things which can be done to enter into deeper relations with self, with other persons, with events, and with God, bringing newness of life."[10]

Let us look for a moment at a positive aspect of loneliness. Did you know that loneliness can be a friend to drive you to God? If it weren't for the anguish of loneliness, many of us would lack the incentive to seek the fellowship of God and the comfort of the Holy Spirit. We don't need God as a friend when our lives are filled with meaningful human relationships. The truth is that we seldom have time for God in the busy round of social intercourse.

So, instead of wallowing in the self-pity loneliness generates, do something constructive about it. Self-pity is the first step down the path to depression and suicide. "Self-pity is the one emotion which never did anyone any good . . . that is a road leading to deep loneliness of spirit."[11]

How can self-pity be overcome? Try the following:

1. Confess the sin of self-pity which almost always accompanies the feeling of loneliness.

2. Forgive those who may be causing you hurt by rejecting you.

3. Ask God to reveal any temperament weaknesses that may be keeping people from accepting you.
4. Ask God to teach you a new dependence on Him so that He can be the Friend you really need.
5. Renew your commitment to the Lord and determine by His grace to make Him the object and center of your life.

Now let's consider three temperament traits that invariably lead to loneliness. You may be a Christian, you may be experiencing the Spirit-filled life, you may be doing everything else suggested in this book and still feel lonely and rejected. The reason may be one of the following:

Egotism, or Self-centeredness

If you wish to be miserable, you must think about yourself; about what you want, what you like, what respect people ought to pay you, and then to you nothing will be pure. You will spoil everything you touch; you will make sin and misery out of everything God sends you. You can be as wretched as you choose.[12]

When we are small children, our world is confined to such a limited sphere that it is understandable for a child to exhibit self-centeredness. But as our world broadens to include more people, geographical expanse, and experiences, so should our interests. To remain self-centered in adulthood is to refuse the natural process of growth into maturity. Self-centeredness in children is child*like;* in adults, it is child*ish.* A vast difference!

Let us consider the typical conversation patterns of the self-centered individual:

First of all, he seeks to dominate every conversation. After a few attempts at dialogue, you realize he is not listening—only waiting for a slight pause to rush in and say, "You ought to hear what happened to me!" With that he launches into his own "me"–slanted story and takes over.

When I am involved in this type of one-sided communication, I slip into the mental neutrality of "yes," "m-hmm," "oh, really?"—just waiting to seize an opportunity to say, "It surely has been nice to see you again. Have a great day, and I'll see you later." Then I endeavor to avoid future encounters. Where does that leave the frustrated self-seeker? Alone. Lonely.

Second, he loves to magnify and rehearse every miniscule problem, ache, or pain. He finds peculiar pleasure in inflicting the details of his misfortunes on others. His troubles always exceed those of others.

The truth is that no one wants to know your problems. When I greet a person with "How are you?" I really don't want to hear intimate details. I'm merely using the accepted form of saying "hello." For those who misinterpret this polite exchange to force me into hearing a recitation of personal woes, loneliness for him is the end result.

The egotist also has the mistaken notion that if he can belittle others, he is magically building himself up in the process. Therefore, in some subtle (or otherwise) fashion, he places an undermining suggestion at the psychologically strategic moment, then emerges with a smug feeling of superiority.

Perhaps it would be well here to evaluate your own communication patterns:

How would you rate yourself?	Always	Often	Seldom	Never
1. Do you dominate every conversation?				
2. Do you insist on having the last word?				
3. Must you be right in every disagreement?				

4. Do you listen well?

5. Instead of listening, are you just waiting to speak?

6. Do you try to honestly communicate your true feelings?

7. Is your conversation "I" centered? (If you are not sure, listen to yourself for a few days.)

How did you score in this simple exercise? If you were honest, that is the first step to overcoming your problem. It takes determined effort to defeat ingrained habits, but it can be done.

Remember that God wants you to have victory in this matter of loneliness, but the devil doesn't. You are fighting a very real enemy, but Jesus already has won the battle. The Bible says:

> It is true that I am an ordinary, weak human being, but I don't use human plans and methods to win my battles. I use God's mighty weapons, not those made by men, to knock down the devil's strongholds (2 Cor. 10:3–4 LB).

One of God's most powerful weapons is prayer. He says: ". . . the reason you don't have what you want is that you don't ask God for it" (James 4:2b LB). "Ask, using my name, and you will receive" (John 16:24 LB).

In simple faith, ask God to help you overcome self-centeredness.

We've all been guilty more than we care to admit. The seeds of criticism thus planted begin to grow. The tragedy is that once we have deposited the bad seed and covered it over with the cares of life, its presence and growth occur secretly. Neither we nor anyone else can detect this early putting down of roots. That's why we are warned in the Bible to tear out "roots of bitterness."

Have you ever tried to weed a rock garden? The new little shoots are tender, and the tiny roots can be removed with very little pressure. Neglect to pull those young weeds, however, and you can hardly blast out the mature offenders. Move the surrounding rocks, soak the ground with water, and still you can pull with all your might and fail to extract the entire root. What happens then? The remaining fragment begins to grow and in time produces another weed. Now, however, the root is so deep you almost never reach it.

So it is with a critical spirit. Let that tiny seed grow, and before you realize what has happened, your whole spirit is poisoned. Try to love that person you criticized, and you cannot, no matter how much prayer and effort are exerted. Alienation sets in because people mysteriously sense our spirit. Without anyone telling me, I know if they like me or not. When I sense rejection, I don't stay around. I go where I am accepted—and so do you!

A critical spirit may begin with one or two people, but left to grow within, it spreads like the mustard seed. Eventually we are critical of everyone we meet. Soon we shut out those around us, and we don't even know why. In return, they shut us out, and there we are. All alone, and oh, so lonely!

To eradicate roots of bitterness and a critical spirit is not easy. Many sincere Christians end in despair when they fail again and again. You must determine at the outset that to remove these full-grown roots will take time and perseverance. The steps I am outlining must be applied as long as the disease persists:

1. Give God permission to go to work eradicating this sin, however painful. You can't do it alone (Rom. 12:1–2).

2. Every time you harbor a critical thought, confess it (1 John 1:9).

3. Pray for those people you can't seem to like, and those who dislike you (Matt. 5:44).

4. Begin to reach out with love as God starts the healing process (1 Peter 4:8 LB).

A NEGATIVE OUTLOOK

This is probably the most difficult of the temperament problems to overcome because usually we had nothing to do with its existence. Long before we were conscious of negative or positive attitudes, our parents and home environment programmed us to react negatively in life's situations. Many people are hardly aware of this personality weakness.

Let me illustrate by a conversation I recently heard between an apartment manager and an older resident of the building. I call this:

The Saga of Mamie's Miseries

Manager: "Mamie, you look a little down today. What seems to be the matter?"

Mamie: "Oh, I don't know. Nobody seems to like me. I don't have any friends—nothing to do. I'm old and all alone in my apartment. Even my children won't come to see me."

Manager: "Have you ever thought about volunteer work, Mamie? There's so much opportunity to help others."

Mamie: "No. I can't do anything. Besides, who would listen to me? Nobody talks to me. Nobody cares what I do."

Manager: "But you know, Mamie, there are so
           many people in the world much
           worse off than you are. What about
           old people? You could read to them."

Mamie: "Certainly not! I can't stand old
           people."

Manager: "What about children then? There are
           hundreds of neglected children who
           need love and attention."

Mamie: "Children? Absolutely not! I don't like
           to be around children. They make me
           nervous."

Manager: "You could get a volunteer job in a
           hospital, Mamie. I've talked to lots of
           women who do that, and they just
           love it."

Mamie: "I've already told you I can't do any-
           thing."

Manager: (weary by now and running out of
           suggestions) "Why don't you go to
           college, Mamie? Lots of mature
           people are continuing their education
           and finding new meaning to life."

Mamie: "Naw, I don't want to waste my
           time."

The above drama may sound exaggerated and fic-
tionalized, but it is a duplication of an actual conversation.
Even Mamie's name remains unchanged. She is representa-
tive of thousands of people who have become bitter, caustic,
and complaining. Unbearably lonely, too.

Mamie can't understand why the clerks at the grocery
store, post office, and every shop she patronizes dread to see
her come. She's right, too. No one can tolerate being around

her, including her children. Instead of asking "why," however, she merely drones on and on with her complaining.

Our hearts ache for the Mamies of this world, but they didn't get that way overnight. They often started down that road at a relatively early age, as suggested above. By the time most people march to the wedding altar, they are so proficient at creative complaining that they can sour every circumstance of life, including those designed to be joyous.

Their cop-out is, "I'm just a realist. I look at things as they really are." With that statement, they squelch anyone with a positive outlook and further conceal the hidden malady that keeps them miserable and lonely.

A negative, complaining spirit poisons many a relationship and terminates countless friendships and marriages. Medical doctors and researchers are telling us that bottled-up resentments and negative reactions to stress cause degenerative diseases. Even Plato said, "All diseases of the body proceed from the mind or soul."

Let's face it. Everyone prefers the company of happy, hopeful, positive people. A negative spirit is contagious, but so is a positive one. We have a choice. If we select for our friends and associates those who drag us down with their dismal attitude, we become depressed and life appears hopeless.

The sad thing is that our society seems geared to the negative. Take the weather forecast, for instance. We hear, "There is a 20 percent chance of showers." What about the 80 percent possibility of no showers? We listen to these reports and start looking for the slim margin of bad weather. Transfer that spirit to all of life, and in every situation we watch for the 20 percent chance of misfortune. So we're constantly expecting the worst.

The Bible commands us over and over to defeat negativism and maintain a positive attitude:

> "Do all things without murmurings and disputings" (Phil. 2:14).

"Rejoice in the Lord always . . ." (Phil. 4:4).
"In every thing give thanks . . ." (1 Thess. 5:18).
"All things work together for good . . ." (Rom. 8:28).

This is a tough assignment, but it will prove to be one of the most decisive actions in the battle against loneliness, so it's worth every effort. Few of us escape the need for constant vigilance in this war against negativism, for we have to guard our spirits lest they be influenced by those around us, or our adverse circumstances, or the tendency of the world system to magnify the bad and minimize the good.

What can you do?

1. Ask God every day, many times a day, to give you the strength and desire to maintain a positive attitude.

2. Consciously remove yourself from negative people. If they live with you in the same house, this is impossible, of course. If they don't, stay away from them during the learning period at least.

3. Consciously choose to be around positive people. Remember, both negative and positive attitudes are contagious.

4. Thank God for every circumstance, every person, and every detail of your life. The more you exercise yourself in obedience to 1 Thessalonians 5:18, the sooner "all things work together for good" in your behalf.

5. Refuse the temptation to have to understand the reason for the things that are happening to you before you can thank God for them. Sometimes, understanding is a great hindrance to believing. Besides, if God is lovingly arranging your circumstances for your good and His glory, why do you have to understand?

Epilogue

To sift through the memories of a lifetime in order to write a book can be depressingly painful. Especially as those memories relate to loneliness. I cannot say that such pain has been absent from the preparation and writing of this book. Quite the contrary. As forgotten incidents emerged into the light, again I relived their agony. I saw more clearly mistakes I had made which I did not recognize at the time. I felt again the old waves of loneliness and meaninglessness sweeping over me.

But that was not all. Simply to remember those past heartaches would prove fruitless if reliving the pain was all I had gained. I don't like to hurt that much. From it, however, I learned that pushing unpleasant experiences into the subconscious is no answer to loneliness. Refusing to admit that I am lonely doesn't help either. And refusing to deal squarely with the issues by rationalization or procrastination is not an escape. All of these methods merely complicate my search for wholeness and hide the solutions I am seeking.

How to resolve unresolved issues and work my way through the problem of loneliness, I discovered, was a lengthy process. The principles I have shared in this book cover a period of several years of perseverence, of stumbling and falling and picking myself up again, and of determining to win. The psalmist declared:

> The steps of a good man are ordered by the LORD; and he delighteth in his way. Though he fall, he shall not be utterly cast down: for the LORD upholdeth him with his hand . . . none of his steps shall slide (Ps. 37:23–24, 31).

It is one thing to begin well, but it is quite another to end well. The process involves getting up every time you fall. And the faster you get up to start again, the sooner you'll reach the finish line and experience victory.

There are no hopeless cases in God's eyes. Remember Jose and Juanita? Humanly speaking, they didn't have a ghost of a chance, did they? Yet today they are reaping the fruit of the eternal seeds planted when they recognized their lost condition and reached out for God's remedy for hopeless cases. You should see them now. They have a beautiful, loving relationship, and are active in church with their two children following their godly example. They are leading lives of useful service to the Lord and mankind. *If God could change Jose and Juanita,* who were at the absolute bottom, *He can change you, too.*

As we read the Bible, we discover a startling fact. Almost all of the people within its pages were lonely. There is a reason for that, and when we begin to understand that reason, we can deal with loneliness a little better. The following story explains what I mean:

An older couple who had been missionaries for years were returning home for furlough on a huge ship. They had given all their lives seeking to win to Christ the inhabitants of a culture far different from their own. They were worn out and broken in health.

On the same ship was a group of youthful entertainers who had gone to that same country for a month of concert touring. A large crowd of people and a band jammed the docks to welcome the young people home. Not a soul was there to greet the old missionaries.

"It just doesn't seem fair," the dear, old man complained to his wife. "We've given all our lives in selfless service and no one is here to even greet us."

She reached over and patted his hand. "Don't worry about it, dear. We're not home yet, you know."

The old missionary couple knew where home for them really was, and they had been heading in that direction all their earthly pilgrimage. The same is true for us. Our *real* home is in heaven. In that beautiful place we will experience *perfect* joy, *perfect* peace, and *perfect* happiness.

Meanwhile, there is good news for God's lonely children on their way to heaven. You may be lonely a great deal in this old world. Life may be tough and filled with bitter struggles. Jesus never promised us immunity from trouble. He Himself had more than His fair share. He did promise us, however, that we never have to be alone on our homeward journey. For one thing, Jesus said, "I will never leave you." He also said, "I will ask the Father, and he will give you another [Comforter] to be with you forever." He is the Holy Spirit. . . . So Jesus gave us the joy of His companionship, the light of His Word, the communion of prayer, and the sweet fellowship of His body.

> When we walk with the Lord
> In the light of His Word,
> What a glory He sheds on our way

is not just to be sung. It is a way of life meant for us to enjoy every day until we reach our eternal home.

Lonely? Maybe. But never alone!

If you would like to get in touch with Nicky he can be reached at:

Nicky Cruz Outreach
P.O. Box 1330
Colorado Springs, CO 80901

Notes

Prologue

[1]Wolfe, Thomas. "American Mercury," October, 1941.

Chapter 1

[1]Tanner, Ira J. *Loneliness: The Fear of Love,* New York: Harper & Row, 1973, p. 3.
[2]Cruz, Nicky. *Run Baby Run,* Plainfield, New Jersey: Logos, 1968, p. 19.

Chapter 2

[1]Rosenbaum, Jean and Veryl. *Conquering Loneliness,* New York: Hawthorn Books, 1973, p. 146.
[2]Cruz, *Run Baby Run,* pp. 23, 28.
[3]Cruz, *Run Baby Run,* p. 100.

Chapter 3

[1]Cruz, *Run Baby Run,* p. 111.
[2]Cruz, *Run Baby Run,* p. 114.
[3]Cruz, *Run Baby Run,* p. 114.
[4]Cruz, *Run Baby Run,* p. 114.
[5]Cruz, *Run Baby Run,* p. 115.

Chapter 4

[1]Rosenbaum, *Conquering Loneliness,* p. 145.

Chapter 5

[1]Johnson, James L. *Loneliness Is Not Forever,* Chicago: Moody Press, 1979, p. 122.
[2]Slater, Philip. *The Pursuit of Loneliness,* Boston: Beacon Press, 1976, p. 6.
[3]Lauder, Robert E. *Loneliness Is for Loving,* Notre Dame, Indiana: Ave Maria Press, 1978, p. 10.

Chapter 7

[1]Graham, Billy. *The Holy Spirit,* Waco, Texas: Word Books, 1978, p. 98.

[2]Graham, *The Holy Spirit,* p. 99.

[3]Wirt, Sherwood Eliot. *Freshness of the Spirit,* San Francisco: Harper & Row, 1978, p. 73.

[4]Cruz, *Run Baby Run,* p. 150.

[5]Nee Watchman. *Twelve Baskets Full,* Los Angeles: The Stream Publishers, 1966, p. 146.

[6]Nee, *Twelve Baskets,* p. 148.

Chapter 9

[1]Lee, Mark W. *How to Have a Good Marriage,* Chappaqua, New York: Christian Herald Books, 1978, p. 49.

[2]Meredith, Don. *Becoming One,* New York: Thomas Nelson, Publishers, 1979, p. 18.

[3]Meredith, *Becoming One,* p. 18.

[4]Chavez, Patricia. *Picking Up the Pieces,* Nashville: Thomas Nelson Publishers, 1979, p. 128.

[5]Chavez, *Picking Up,* p. 130.

[6]Mains, Karen Burton. *The Key to a Loving Heart,* Elgin, Illinois: David C. Cook Publishing Co., 1979, p. 130.

[7]Mains, *The Key,* p. 130.

[8]Chavez, *Picking Up,* p. 131.

[9]Chavez, *Picking Up,* p. 131.

Chapter 10

[1]Johnson, *Loneliness Is Not Forever,* p. 87.

[2]Johnson, *Loneliness Is Not Forever,* p. 87.

[3]Wood, Margaret Mary. *Paths of Loneliness,* New York: Columbia University Press, 1953, p. 78.

[4]Meredith, *Becoming One,* pp. 206–207.

Chapter 11

[1]Mains, *The Key,* p. 145.

Chapter 12

[1]Tanner, *Loneliness, Fear,* p. 9.

[2]Potthoff, Harvey H. *Loneliness: Understanding and Dealing With It,* Nashville: Abingdon, 1976, p. 14.

[3]Tanner, *Loneliness, Fear,* p. x Introduction.

[4]Tanner, *Loneliness, Fear,* p. 71.

[5]Potthoff, *Loneliness: Understanding,* p. 14.

[6]Potthoff, *Loneliness: Understanding,* p. 14.

[7]Warlick, Harold C., Jr. *Conquering Loneliness*, Waco, Texas: Word Books, 1979, p. 25.

[8]Tanner, *Loneliness, Fear*, p. 71.

[9]Potthoff, *Loneliness: Understanding*, p. 12.

[10]Potthoff, *Loneliness: Understanding*, p. 109.

[11]Potthoff, *Loneliness: Understanding*, p. 56.

[12]Osborne, Cecil, *The Art of Understanding Yourself*, Grand Rapids: Zondervan, 1967, p. 9.